DAUGHTER OF THE MOUNTAINS

DAUGHTER
of the
MOUNTAINS

by Louise Rankin

ILLUSTRATED BY KURT WIESE

THE VIKING PRESS · NEW YORK

FIC   I.   INDIA

       2.   TIBET

CONTENTS

I. The Gift of a Red-Gold Lhasa Terrier 11

II. Adventure! The Beginning of the Prophecy 38

III. The Giant Staircase and the Forest 57

IV. Captured by the Woman at Rhenok 79

V. The Ten Traders and Tsu Foo 102

VI. Protector of the Poor 125

VII. Lotus Blossom's Plan 149

VIII. Fulfillment of the Prophecy: Good Fortune 168

ILLUSTRATIONS

Fine views spread out before them the whole of their small high world 10

A horde of demons came rushing out into the court 13

Choosing a central spot under the feet of the Blessed One, Momo set down her offering 23

A young lama with calm eyes stood before them and spoke to Muni 25

There was nothing so fine to see and hear as this coming on of
    a mule team   30–31

In the hollow of his big hand, Urtken held a golden puppy   34

Tossing a few stones upon the cairn about the prayer flag, she
    made a prayer to the guardian country gods   47

She playfully pummeled the great yak   59

She leaped nimbly down the mountain, leaving the giant stair-
    case to the wool train   65

Two half-grown pigs nearly knocked Momo over   71

The farther she went, the more the bamboo poles swayed   85

"She's teaching the children to swing from one tree to another" 93

She fell and went coasting down the hillside through the mud   97

Momo sat in a ball and thought only of sleep   99

Momo had never seen people carry things like this before   107

She was fascinated by the Indian bankers   113

A girl, coming out, stumbled and fell over Momo   116

Momo leaped to safety as the great black beast or demon whizzed
    past   121

All the people standing respectfully before the tall British gen-
    tleman were thrown into a heap   130

"My lord the tiger comes out in the early dawn"   137

This, the sunset, was the time for prayer   139

Close on Big Dorje's heels, Momo climbed into a carriage   143

Suddenly his foot shot out, his hand snatched at the scarf   148

Momo sat down on the temple steps   155

The Chinese turned and smiled at her   161

She sank to the floor and sat there, hugging Pempa to her   181

FOREWORD

Like a great pear hanging from the mainland of Asia lies the
wonderful land of India. Along the northern, or stem, end of
this pear the high Himalayas, mightiest mountains of the
world, both connect India to Asia and shut it off. But not by
an unbroken barrier; for a few narrow passes open a way into
India's rich and sunny plains.

And through these passes, from time out of mind, have
poured the armies of invaders, Chinese, Turkomen, and, over
the famed Khyber Pass, the great Mohammedan conquerors.
Last came the traders from over the sea. While America was
being settled adventurers from Portugal, France, and England
were sailing off to trade with India. Gradually the English won

this rich field for themselves alone and took over the government of the land.

The people of India have either absorbed their conquerors or worked by peaceful means for their freedom. And now, in our own time, it has come! On August 15, 1947, two dominions, Pakistan for the Mohammedans, Hindustan for the Hindus, were created free and independent.

Within these two countries are many different kinds of people, speaking hundreds of different languages, living by different customs. For under any and all governments the wise men of India have believed in leaving people free to think and to live as they please; and that is the greatest fascination of India—her people and their age-old individualities and beliefs. As you will see in this story of Momo, whose adventures took place in the last years of the British rule in India.

DAUGHTER OF THE MOUNTAINS

I. THE GIFT OF A RED-GOLD LHASA TERRIER

Ever since she could remember, Momo had wanted a dog. But no ordinary cur, such as she might easily have got, would do. She had set her heart on a very special kind of dog—a red-gold Lhasa terrier. There was one at the Kargayu monastery; it belonged to the head *lama* (priest). And from the moment when she had first seen this dog, Momo had one passionate longing —to have, for her very own, a red-gold terrier from Lhasa.

She was only four years old on that day. Nema, her father,

had swung her up onto his shoulder and had set off with his family for the Red Hat festival at Kargayu. They were all very merry; for her father, who carried the mail over the mountains, and her mother, who kept a little tea shop in their home, worked very hard, and a holiday was a great thing. And so was the festival! For three days they and all the countryside would watch the lamas' dances, and eat the good food and drink the strong tea of the monastery.

From every house and hamlet other families came out to join them, until a gay procession was streaming down the mountainside. All but the smallest children walked; for in far-off Tibet, where there are no cars nor trains, and only the rich have mules or horses to ride, the people walk. They wear high red felt boots, and climb with a quick, springing step up and down their high mountains, forty or fifty miles a day, thinking no more of it than the eagle does of soaring through air.

When they came to the monastery, Momo's two brothers ran quickly into the courtyard and found themselves places in the front row. And though they were on the side set apart for the poor people, they were just opposite the raised platform of the head lama. The festival began with a solemn procession, when the lamas, in gorgeous silk robes, went round and round the courtyard. Then the head lama took his place on the platform; there was a shrill bugle cry, and the play began.

"Have no fear, Momo," said her father, putting his strong arms about his little daughter. "These are not real demons; they are the good lamas of the monastery, with masks over their faces."

As he spoke, the music changed from a low wailing to furious trumpet blasts, and a horde of demons, with fearful faces, came rushing out into the court. Everybody sucked in his breath, and

pressed closer to his neighbor. For the Tibetans had lived in terror of such evil spirits until a Buddhist priest came up out of India long ago, and taught them Buddha's message of love and kindness. And still the people feared the demons, although the priests reminded them every year, in this three-day long play, that the Lord Buddha's power was great enough to drive away the demons that had tortured them.

"Don't be afraid, little one," repeated Nema, cuddling his child close in his arms. But Momo was not looking at the demons; she did not hear their blood-curdling cries, nor see their malignant faces as they whirled about in a devil dance. She was looking at the dog that sat beside the head lama.

"Father," she said, pointing to the platform, "what is that beside the head lama?"

"Oh," he replied, surprised, "that is his little dog."

Momo still stared fixedly. "But I never saw a dog like that," she said.

Her father laughed and stroked her cheek. "You have seen only common village curs, little Momo," he answered. "That dog is like a prince among men. He is a terrier from our holy capital, Lhasa." The music dropped to a low, sad, wailing note.

"Now see!" he added cheerfully. "These skeletonlike ghosts who flit about the court are not real ghosts, my child. They will not hurt you. They are only the lamas, dressed like that to show us how evil spirits tortured our souls before we learned to pray to the blessed Lord Buddha for deliverance from them." He fingered a little charm box that hung around his neck, and murmured a prayer, looking fearfully at the sad lost souls, and the demons driving them. But Momo made no answer. She had eyes only for the wonderful dog.

He was not too big, not too small, but just right in size. Long silky hair like burnished red gold clothed him in a royal mantle, turned his arching tail into a plume, and dropped over his face like a fringe. He was so beautiful that Momo could hardly believe he was real. But as she watched, she saw that he was very much alive. He sat up and begged for bits of rice cake, which his master tossed him; then he barked and waved his paw in thanks. When anyone came up to speak to the head lama, he stretched out his forepaws, and laid his head on them, bowing low. Then sitting up, he would seem to listen, cocking his head this way and that. And sometimes he would toss his head back so that the golden fringe parted, and showed his eyes, black and keen and merry.

All that day and the second and the third day, Momo watched the dog and not the play. And when the great festival came to an end, and the worshipers rose shouting *"Mangalam!"* (All happiness!) and went in cheerful procession back to their homes, Momo carried with her the image of the golden dog.

She never forgot it, never stopped wanting it. When she was old enough to walk with her mother to the monastery twice a month to pray, she nearly always saw the dog, and every sight of him increased her desire. And after her two little brothers had been given to the monastery to become lamas, she longed for it more than ever. The little wooden doll her father carved out for her was stiff and stupid; now that she was alone in the house, it seemed very dark and empty. In the evening, when her father sat at home, she would go to him, and lean against his knee.

"Father," she would say, "I want a dog."

"A dog?" he would say, pretending to be surprised. "But we have a dog." And so they had. Like every family in Tibet they kept a watchdog, a fierce, unfriendly mastiff that lay like a shaggy doormat before their house even in the deepest winter snows, and barked furiously when anyone came near.

"But," Momo would say, "I want a dog of my very own."

"Oh, well then!" her father would go on, still playing the game of being surprised. "Where did I see puppies—at the house of Pasang?"

"No, no!" Momo would cry. "I don't want that kind. I want a terrier from Lhasa, with long golden hair, like the head lama's dog at the monastery."

And then poor Nema would sigh. He would cheerfully have cut off all the hair in his precious pigtail to give his only daughter pleasure; but although he risked his life crossing over the snowy Jelep La pass to carry the mail, he got paid barely enough to feed his family. And a terrier such as Momo wanted could not be had for nothing. So he would sigh, and stroke her hair and then say cheerfully, "When your uncle comes from Lhasa, he will bring you a dog from there."

"Like the red-gold one with long hair and black eyes at the Kargayu monastery?" Momo would ask.

"Yes, that is the kind he will bring," her father would say. Every night Momo fell asleep dreaming of the golden dog whose bright black eyes flashed out from a mop of hair. But the days and the years passed by, and her uncle never came; by the time Momo was eight years old she could no longer remember what he looked like, this uncle who had gone off to Lhasa, and he too became a dream, like the silky dog he never brought her.

"My uncle never comes," Momo said to her mother. "Shall I never get a terrier from Lhasa?"

"Everything depends on the will of God," her gentle mother replied. "Pray to Him. If the blessed Lord Buddha wishes, He will bring you one."

So Momo began to pray. Every morning and evening she took up the round prayer wheel her father had got from the Red Hat priests of the monastery, and twirled it in one hand as she helped her mother to keep up the fire. Their prayer wheel was only a small copper cylinder on a wooden handle, but inside it was stuffed with a thousand prayers, written in bold black letters in the lamas' careful hand, and blessed by the head lama himself. As she kept the wheel revolving, Momo thought with satisfaction, "Now not only the one prayer of my mouth, but all these thousand prayers reach the ear of the Lord Buddha at the same time." She waited more patiently, believing that He would one day hear these prayers and answer them.

Of still greater power were her visits to the monastery. There Momo made her prayer first inside the temple before the golden image of the Buddha. Then, leaving her mother, whose voice sounded in the great hall like the soft murmuring of a bird about to sleep, Momo would slip out to the big prayer wheel in the courtyard.

This was a wonder wheel indeed. It stood like a tower by the gate, brightly painted with the stories of the Buddha's life, and His priests' conquest of the demons, and it was filled with prayers. Not two hundred, but two hundred thousand times the patient lamas had copied out that prayer, all-powerful to the Buddhists of Tibet: *Om Mani Padme Hum.* And when Momo turned the handle, she knew that the wheel inside the brightly painted walls would lift all these two hundred thousand prayers. They would fly—and the prayer of her heart with them—straight into the ear of the Great Compassionate One. Momo had great faith in this wheel—far greater than in her praying before the temple image.

"For," she thought, "the Blessed One Himself is in the blue

sky far away, and my voice is small. But surely all these prayers of the lamas' holy writing, blessed too by the head lama, and rising from this holy place—surely they will carry my little prayer with them to His ears!"

So with great diligence she had prayed. Nothing happened. He had not heard. At last Momo grew desperate, even angry. She was nine years old, and over. "If I am ever to get the dog," she told herself, "it must be *now*." Summer was passing fast, and soon the long winter would be upon them, when she and her mother would not be able to go to the monastery to pray.

"I will wait until the autumn," Momo decided. "Then, if I still haven't got the dog, I will *make* Him hear me." So through the summer she waited and brooded and made careful plans. And when the summer rains were over, and the skies grew clear again, the nights were cold, and frost colored the leaves of the forest, Momo was ready. On the day of the next full moon she set out with her mother for their last visit to Kargayu. They went not by the road, but as the crows fly— straight down one mountainside, and up the next, until they came to the great gate. There, as was their custom, they stopped to look about.

The monastery stood boldly crowning a rocky shoulder on the long axis of the mountain, with fine views which spread out before them the whole of their small, high world. Behind them the mountain rose in a murmuring tower of trees, whose oaks and maples were like red and yellow fire among the green pines. Off to the south they looked down over the steep way they had come, into the foaming waters of the Chumbi river; tracing its channel up the mountain, they found its source in the snow cap of the Jelep La, shining against the blue sky. And close to the snowy crest of this great mountain Momo could make out every house in their little village of Longram. But beyond this broad sweep of the Jelep La's flank they could not see, for another high mountain closed them in, and marked the boundary line between Tibet and Bhutan.

Eastward, where the monastery faced, to catch the first rays of the morning sun, they looked down upon the flat stone-laden roofs of Rinchengong, and the pleasant Chumbi valley. Here the jade-green Amo river ran merrily between bordering fields of millet, emerald green, and the mountains behind were a vast straight wall in scarlet, gold, and green.

All about them the air was moving in gentle currents, now drifting down sun-warmed and piny from the tree-tops, now rising cool and bittersweet from the frosted flowers underfoot. Standing with the mountain at its back, Kargayu was protected from the fiercest blasts of wind, and the air was always milder there than elsewhere. Momo and her mother took the gentle, drifting breezes as the first blessing of the holy place. Though they had made pilgrimages far over the mountains and the great plain of Tibet, there was no monastery they loved so much as this.

It was not grand, like the great cathedral at Lhasa, and it was not gloriously remote and hard to reach, like many of the monasteries. Momo would never forget climbing by a ladder into Shergol, whose buildings were cut out of the sheer face of a cliff, with only the sky above her, and the deep abyss below; nor the hard exciting journey across dangerous glaciers, in a long line of pilgrims, toiling black spots in this dazzling world of ice, to reach Kye-lang, high on a solitary peak.

But Momo and her mother loved Kargayu all the more, because it was not grand, but gentle and homelike. It was old and holy, and so close to the Chumbi valley towns and the little mountain villages that people need not wait for the big festivals to make a pilgrimage. On every auspicious day, and in all their troubles, they could come to pray.

"Come, Momo," said her mother, turning from the view, "we cannot stay too long, for the caravans must be on the move. Perhaps they are now knocking on our door. And today I have so many prayers to make." She sighed.

On this day of the full moon, at the beginning of autumn, she made all the petitions for the long winter. Not until the snows had fallen and melted from the mountains would she be free to come here again; she would be busy in the little tea shop in her home. So today she prayed first to the Lord Buddha, the Great Compassionate One, to guard her husband Nema in his daily climb with the mails over the top of the Jelep La pass, and to save him from death by freezing or falling into treacherous snow drifts. She prayed for the success of her tea shop, for their health, and she prayed that they might all be true followers of the Way.

"Today we must be quick. Come," she said again, turning toward the temple. But Momo, whose prayers today were even more urgent than her mother's, had run across the court, and stood on the threshold of the temple. There for a moment she forgot her plans. For always, at this first glimpse within the temple, her heart swelled almost to bursting with the wonder of the place. Then quickly she went in.

After the sunshine of the courtyard, the windowless temple, lighted only from the open doors, plunged her into a sudden twilight. She walked in its dimness to the altar where three great gold images were palely gleaming; she breathed the age-old smell of incense and of butter, burned in offering; she felt rather than saw the richly colored paintings on the walls, brilliant in the light by the door, dimmed elsewhere, but show-ing still the gods, and demons writhing under the lamas' power.

Past the parallel rows of benches where the lamas sat for wor-ship, under the prayer banners hanging from painted beam and pillar, she came slowly to the altar, where the Three Rarest Ones were sitting. The twelve-foot image of the Buddha towered above his two life-sized companions. He sat in the lotus pose, His smooth, great gold legs crossed beneath Him, the hands lying one upon the other, as if in meditation; and on His face and in His eyes a look of absolute peace.

Momo examined the rice heaped in a silver *tali* before the Buddha, and the row of little bowls, shining bright as gold and filled with clear water, that stretched across the brocaded silk cover of the altar. Then choosing a central spot under the feet of the Blessed One, she set down her offering. It was an empty bottle. And in its bulging neck—most wonderful to see—a glass marble was imprisoned. This was Momo's treasure, and her only possession. Pasang, who had found it, agreed to trade her the bottle if she would watch his mother's ducks for two months. Even after she had done so, he was reluctant to let the treasure go, until he fell ill of a fever which his mother blamed on the demon in the bottle.

Assuredly there was magic in the bottle. That the children knew from merely looking at the glass marble which could not be shaken out of its bulging neck. But what the bottle was for, or why the marble was there, they could not guess until Nema, who knew everything, explained.

"Oh, yes," said he. "This is the magic of the English—white-faced folk, whom, along with all foreign unbelievers, we forbid entrance into our holy land of Tibet. The bottle is for soda water. By their magic this marble and this wire clamp hold the demon in the water till the clamp is lifted. Then," he added impressively, and making a wry face, "both demon and water rush out like the foaming torrents of melting snow; and if you drink, it fills your nose with a sharp pain."

Momo had set the bottle in the corner where her mother made the family altar, and never tired of marveling at it, or rolling the marble around, to see how cleverly it did not fall out. Not without a wrench, but with great devotion, she now gave it to the Blessed One. Then, tilting her head far back, to look up into the still yellow face of the Buddha, she said her prayer with all the intensity of her heart. And having said it, she bowed before the altar, then turned and went quickly out to the great prayer wheel.

Here, as he had promised, she found little Muni, her younger brother, holding the head lama's dog by a leash. Without a word or a glance for her brother, Momo grasped the handle of the wheel.

"Today," she thought, "I will beat my prayers into His ears, like a traveler making a forced journey in the night, who knocks upon the door of the tea house, and does not fear the dogs, but keeps on hammering and hammering at the door until he wakes the sleeping house, and then demands his tea. Today my prayers must strike upon the ear of the Blessed One like a heavy blow, strong enough to *make* Him hear."

So she fixed her eyes on the dog, and all the strength of her mind on her wish. "*Om Mani Padme Hum!*" Her lips murmured the prayer. The wheel, for all its size, turned lightly in her hand. When it had come full circle a bell rang, a solemn, measured tone in the tranquil air. Momo drew a deep breath and began again. Again the bell rang, a different note. Again and yet again the wheel went round. The little boy priest, with

his plum-colored robe and close-cropped head, stood quietly holding the dog; the dog sat quietly looking at Momo. Momo's black eyes stared unwinking at the precious dog.

"*Om Mani Padme Hum! Om Mani Padme Hum!*" The words raced through her brain, and tumbled from her lips. Faster and faster she twirled the handle, faster and faster the wheel went spinning, faster and louder the bells kept ringing. With every peal, fresh echoes woke around the courtyard and came rushing back in jumbled waves of sound, muffling the bells' clear peal, filling the court with clangor and confusion.

"What is this, brother?" A young lama with calm eyes stood before them, and spoke to Muni, who looked up at him.

"At this time," he replied, "His Holiness, the head lama, meditates alone, and I keep the dog for him." The young priest nodded. He too had once been the youngest in the monastery, and he knew that the kindly old head lama liked to give the youngest child-monk the pleasure of caring for his pet dog.

"But why do you stand here? Who is this?" The lama nodded toward Momo, who was still making the handle fly, so intent on her prayers that she heard and saw nothing.

"That is Momo, my sister," said little Muni. "She wants a dog like this one of the head lama, so she asked me to bring it here before her."

The lama laid a hand gently on Momo's shoulder. "And why," he asked, "turn the wheel so often and so hard, my child? Do you not know that worshipers give it only a couple of twists?"

With a start Momo stopped and stared at the lama.

"A-a-a-ah!" she sighed, all the air of her lungs coming out softly, like a balloon that is pricked. The lama repeated his question.

"I want a dog like this," said Momo, "and I have prayed so long and He does not hear me. But I have been too gentle; to-day I am hard, and I am making noise enough to wake Him, sleeping in the distant heavens. Today I must *make* Him hear."

At this moment her mother stepped out of the temple, and came running toward them.

"Oh, Oh!" she cried. "What—" But the lama raised his hand, stopping her.

"No harm," he said. "It is a child's longing, but she understands the secret of prayer." He turned again to Momo.

"The prayers in the wheel, little Momo," he observed, "bring us worshipers of the Holy Religion deliverance from the evil of rebirth. Pray to Mother Tara, the Goddess of Mercy, for the small desires of this life." Momo's face fell; and seeing her distress, the lama added kindly, "You have done well, child. Only, as you grow bigger, pray less for the little things of this life, and more for the attainment of birth in the western heaven. So you may be delivered from the wheel of things." He dropped his eyes and murmured a prayer, his hand steadily twirling the prayer wheel he held.

"But the dog?" Momo asked fearfully.

The lama looked up and smiled at her. "Surely your wish is fulfilled, child," he replied. "Is it not written that there is never failure for the worshiper who like a highwayman forces himself upon the Enlightened One?"

Momo clasped her hands and bowed before the young lama. "Oh, great mercy," she cried. "Bless you, bless you—may all your desires be fulfilled, may your merit reach perfection!" He smiled again and walked quickly away, leaving Momo to rush up to Muni and her mother.

"Did you hear?" she cried. "My wish is granted. He has

heard my prayer. Oh, I am so happy, so happy!" She seized her brother by the hand and danced about with him, the dog entering into the fun and capering with them, while her mother smiled to see their joy.

"Come, come," she said at last. "We are late." She said a tender farewell to her small son, and hurried Momo out of the courtyard, through the great gate of the monastery, and down the mountainside. As they came near their village Momo found Pasang out on the road, trying to catch his fat mother duck, that was always running away to paddle in the Chumbi river.

"Ho, Pasang!" she shouted. "My wish is granted! I am to get the dog!"

"Huh!" he grunted, making a dive after the duck. "Come and help me catch her." This was never easy, for the old duck was expert at slipping out of their outstretched hands. "How does the dog come to you?" asked Pasang curiously.

"How should I know?" replied Momo. "Perhaps the Holy One sends it through the air with a guard of country gods."

"Or it may come with the caravans," replied Pasang, more matter-of-factly. "They are gathering, my father said last night." For a moment both children were silent, thinking with joy of the coming excitement; for wool is the great trade of Tibet, and their little village lay on the Great Trade Route between Tibet and India.

Through the summer herdsmen high in the mountains and plains of Tibet cut the thick wool from their flocks. Then, when the heavy rains of the Indian monsoon season are over, they send this thick, fine wool into the wool-trading towns. Here the muleteers, men of Khamba province, tall and immensely strong, are waiting to load it onto the backs of their mules. And then the caravans begin their long march across the lofty

Tibetan plateau, the Roof of the World, over the mountains of the Himalayas, the highest in the world, down into the plains of India.

All the caravans stopped in Momo's village to rest their mules, because, after leaving Longram, they would begin the last terribly steep climb to the eastern boundary of Tibet, at the top of the Jelep La pass. And while the mules rested, the men would come into Momo's house to drink tea. Because of the caravans Momo loved the winter. As soon as the skies cleared in autumn and the sun shone on woods turning yellow and scarlet she would listen eagerly for the first silvery tinkle of the mule trains.

To give warning to oncoming travelers over the mountain passes every mule in a train is belled, and every train has a leader who wears not one, but a whole collar of bells. Whether they are of brass or bell metal, or only of iron, the bells are always clear in tone, and their mingled notes float through the air like sweet music. Long before Momo's sharp eyes could see a mule train moving up through the forested mountainside, she would hear these bells chiming. Now, even while she and Pasang were lunging after the fat old duck, and shouting with laughter to see it slip out of their grasp, shaking its white tail feathers and quacking angrily at them, Momo was listening. Suddenly above their laughter she heard a different sound, and caught her breath. It was—yes, it *was* the music of the mule bells—faint, still far away, but clearly ringing.

Jumping to her feet, forgetting the duck, leaving Pasang to gape, she rushed up the path to her home, shouting as she went.

"Mother! Here they come—they are coming!" Her mother smiled at her and said, "Then come quickly to churn the tea, while I get some cheese and curds ready." So Momo ran over to the churn, which was so high that she had to stand on a stool to reach its plunger. Her mother poured in the strong, black tea which had been brewing on the stove, added some salt and soda, some butter, and some boiling water. Then Momo pushed the plunger up and down as hard and fast as she could.

Meanwhile her mother took one of the strings of smoked cheese off the peg where they hung and pushed the dried pieces, like brown beads, off the string into a pan of warm water to soften them. These dried cheese beads are *tsampa*, made by the wandering Tibetan herdsmen from the milk of their yaks; and if a poor Tibetan can have these to suck, and as many cups of hot buttered tea as he wants in a day—fifty or sixty would not be too many—he is content. Next Momo's mother turned out a dish of curds and whey that had been standing on the back of the stove, and set it on the table.

"Good!" she said, taking the plunger from Momo. "I'll finish this and pour it into the pots. Go and see them come." And Momo ran to the door to watch the lead mule climb into sight.

"Ah!" she murmured, her eyes shining with joy. "Ah!" Outside of the monasteries and the dances of the lamas, there was nothing so fine to hear and to see as this coming on of a mule train. The leader carried his pack lightly, proud of his great responsibility of keeping to the trail, and picking the easiest and safest way over boulders or snow drifts. With every step his embroidered bell collar jingled, and its great tassel of red yak hair bobbed gently against his strong shoulders. One by one, scrambling up the stony way, the other mules followed their leader. For every eight or ten mules there was a muleteer, watching to see that the packs did not come loose. They wore high red felt boots and turquoise earrings, and walked with a spring. Momo smiled to see them, for though the men of Khamba are

known to be hot-tempered, like all Tibetans they are cheerful and fond of children.

The mules knew exactly where they were going, and what to do. They gathered in the mule yard by the house, stamping their little feet. "Seventy-nine, eighty," said Momo, counting the mules as they came up. It was a game she always played. "Eighty mules and eight muleteers," she called to her mother.

"Not very big," she thought, for sometimes there would be hundreds of mules in a caravan, "but *the first!*" She watched the muleteers examine their animals to make sure the wooden packs were not cutting sores into their backs, for they take good care of their mules, then smiled as they came stamping into the house, calling out greetings.

"You are the first caravan to come over the pass. Oh, lucky ones!" cried Momo's mother, as she welcomed them. The men

laughed and sat down, pulling their tea cups out of the fold in their blouses. They were in high spirits. To be first going out of Tibet over the narrow mountain passes meant that they would not meet any returning caravans, coming back into Tibet laden with bricks of tea and brocaded silks, after having sold off their wool.

"Lucky indeed, if we escape late rains or early snow!" their leader replied. "We shall certainly not have to fight our way over the mountains." For when two long mule caravans meet on the mountain trails, so narrow that only one mule may pass, the hot-tempered men of Khamba fight fiercely for the right of way. This leader was himself a peaceful man, and hated to bring violence and bloodshed into the quiet mountains.

They waited eagerly for Momo's mother to fill their cups with the steaming hot tea, and dipped into the bowl of tsampa that Momo brought.

"Why, here is Momo," cried the leader, who remembered this little girl, the same age as his own. "How you have grown! You are taller now than my Dolma." He laughed again.

"What do you think my Dolma wanted me to bring her back from the big bazaar at Kalimpong?" he asked them all. " 'Shall I bring you a coral bead, or a turquoise nose drop?' I asked." And in a high, thin falsetto he copied a child's voice. " 'No, no—bring me momo. I want momo.' " He turned to Momo. "Will you come?" he asked.

They all roared with laughter at this. For "Momo" was only a pet name that her father had begun to call her when she was a baby. *Momo* is really a sweet little dumpling, which the Tibetans like to eat better than anything.

"This child cares nothing for sweets," her mother said. "She wants only one thing in all the world—a Lhasa terrier—"

"A *red-gold* Lhasa terrier, Mother," Momo interrupted, and her mother nodded, and sighed.

"Yes, even the color must be as she wishes," she said. "The child turns our prayer wheel by the hour, in the hope that the Enlightened One will hear and grant her wish."

At this Urtken, the leader, looked thoughtfully at Momo.

"How came you, child," he asked, "to set your heart on a red-gold terrier from Lhasa?" And Momo answered simply, "Because the head lama at Kargayu has one such, and I saw it there—Oh so many years ago! and have wanted one like it ever since."

Urtken scratched his chin, and fingered the turquoise in his ear, and sat thinking, like a man trying to make up his mind. Finally he struck his hand upon the table and beckoned Momo to him.

"See what I have here," he said. So Momo went and stood beside him, watching curiously as he fumbled around in the fold of his heavy robe. Both men and women in Tibet wear long heavy woolen robes, which they tie with a cord about their waists, and pull into a big blouse; and in the big pouch made by this folding of the robe they carry everything they own—which is not much.

"See here!" Urtken repeated, drawing his hand out of the fold. And when she saw what he held, Momo caught her breath and clasped her hands. For in the hollow of his big hand, Urtken held a golden puppy! It was fat and sleepy, and so young that its eyes were still blue, and it looked like a ball of golden fuzz.

"See!" said Urtken dramatically. "A red-gold terrier from Lhasa!"

"Ah! A-ah!" Momo sighed, as the mule leader put the

warm little puppy into her outstretched hands. She held it close, and laughed when the puppy licked at her brown cheek, his eyes, so softly blue, close to her own.

"Is he for me?" asked Momo, and she looked imploringly at her mother, hoping that if he was for sale, she would bargain for him.

"What is his price?" asked her mother, coming over from the stove to look carefully at the puppy.

"It should be much," replied Urtken, "for there are no Lhasa terriers in all our land more finely bred. His mother was one of those belonging to our Grand Lama himself, the Gem of Majesty, and I had her of a cousin of mine, who serves in the Potala at Lhasa. But the mother has died on this journey, and I cannot feed and care for this little one on the long way into India. Let us make this bargain: the puppy is yours, Momo, to train and to keep, and when he is grown, he shall sire other fine dogs for me."

Her mother nodded, and Momo gasped for joy, hugging the little creature to her.

"But mind you feed him well," the muleteer said to her mother. "He is worth all the milk and tsampa he can eat."

"He shall be fed as well as if he were a child," Momo's mother promised, and Momo added, "Yes, yes, certainly he shall have all the yak milk and tsampa he can eat."

Then, just as politely as if he were concluding the sale of all the wool in his caravan, Urtken smiled and said, "May good come upon you. May no sickness happen in your home." And Momo and her mother bowed and said, "Thanks, thanks. Great mercy."

"And thanks, great thankfulness, to the Holy One," cried Momo, "who has heard my prayers at last!" Then she forgot everything in the world but this wonderful puppy of hers. All day she was busy making a bed, feeding it warmed yak milk, watching it totter about, or lie quietly asleep near the stove. When her father came in he rejoiced at her happiness.

"What do you call him?" he asked.

Momo was thunderstruck; she had never thought of a name to give the dog she wanted, and names are very important in Tibet. They bring luck. When a child is born the parents call in an astrologer, who studies the position of the stars at the time the child is born. And from those stars which are highest in the heavens at that time he draws up a horoscope, which is a plan of the child's life—telling what will happen, and what its nature will be. Then he advises the parents on names that will be good and suitable. Momo's own name was Pempa, which means "Saturday," the day she was born, and Tsering, which means "May she have long life."

"I have no name," Momo replied to her father. "Let us call in the astrologer."

Her father began to laugh. First he leaned against the door. Then he sat down and rocked back and forth. He laughed and laughed till the tears ran down his face, and his cheeks and stomach muscles were stiff.

"Oh, Oh!" he said to her mother, holding his sides, "was there ever such a child? She wants a horoscope for her *dog*." And he laughed again, "Ho! Ho! Ho!" throwing back his head and crinkling his eyes till they were little slits, and the tears ran down his cheeks and into his mouth.

"No, father, not a horoscope—only a name. It's very important, his name," persisted Momo. And her gentle mother added, "The Enlightened One Himself had a dog, dear to Him."

At this moment a man came in the open door, and Momo rushed forward with a squeal of joy.

"Oh, come in, Dawa, come in!" she cried. "See, father, here is the astrologer himself. We want a name for my new dog," she said quickly to Dawa. "My father laughs at me, and says I am silly. But you don't think I am, do you? He should have an auspicious name, shouldn't he?" She dragged Dawa to see the sleeping puppy. He looked thoughtfully from the puppy to Momo.

"Get me the plan of the child's life," he said. So Momo's mother fetched it from the chest where they kept their few precious belongings, and gave it into Dawa's hands. All three looked with awe at the paper whose lines foretold the life of little Momo, while Dawa studied it in silence. Finally he nodded, pursing up his mouth, rolled it up and gave it back to be put away.

"Yes," he said, "he merits a good name indeed." To the astonished Nema, he added, "You will live to see this dog the bearer of good fortune." Then he turned briskly to Momo. "You got the dog today, you say?" She nodded.

"This is Saturday—Pempa. It is, moreover, the day of the full moon—a most auspicious day. Why not call him Pempa?"

"Oh, yes, of course, it is my name too," said Momo. "That is right."

"It is indeed right," Dawa told her, "that you two be given the same name. For, by the will of the Blessed One, you two will go through many adventures, and this dog will bring fortune to you all."

"What's that you say?" cried Nema. "Fortune to come to us through him? How will he do it? Dig us a treasure?" He laughed at the impossibility of the idea.

"I did not say treasure," replied Dawa severely. "But mark well my words, Nema Tundoop: today adventure and good fortune have come into your house with the dog."

Nema, who intended no disbelief of Dawa's words, was abashed. "May you grow rich," he said thankfully to the astrologer. "Adventure! Fortune! By the Three Rare Ones— coming to *us!* When, Dawa?"

But Dawa merely smiled and said, "Wait and see."

II. ADVENTURE! THE BEGINNING
OF THE PROPHECY

Next morning both Momo and her mother had forgotten
Dawa's words. For Momo, now that she had at last a golden
Lhasa terrier for her very own, could imagine no greater good
fortune in life. And her mother never wished for what she had
not, nor grumbled at what she had; she took each day as it came,
as a gift of the Lord, and was at peace. Only Nema remembered. As he sat at night by their fire he would look
curiously at little Pempa, wondering with a thrill just what
adventures would befall, and when, and what the fortune could
be that this dog would bring them.

But that winter season passed and the fragrant summer came

and passed and nothing happened. Pempa was so well filled
with yak milk that he grew fast from a rolypoly puff ball into a
gangling puppy with long, blundering legs and a voice that
broke and went off into high squeaks when he tried to bark.
When the wool caravans moved in the autumn, Urtken stopped
again at Momo's house.

"Ah!" he said to Momo. "You do take good care of him.
How strong he is! Next year he will be full grown."

And so the second winter came and passed and another summer followed, and still their life went on as before, with neither
adventure nor fortune falling into their hands. But when the
heavy rains of this monsoon season ended Pempa was, as Urtken
had said he would be, full grown and very beautiful. The milk
and cheese he had eaten had made his bones strong and put a
wonderful gloss on his heavy coat. His tail arched gaily over his
back and waved like a beautiful plume. Long golden hair fell
like a curtain over his face, hiding his eyes until they flashed
out merrily when he tossed his head. He was, Momo knew, the
most beautiful dog in the world, and as her father had said of the
head lama's terrier, like a prince among men.

He was as gentle as he was strong, and had fine manners.
Before entering the house in winter he always stopped to shake
the snow from his long, thick hair. He sat up and begged for his
tsampa, and said thank you with a bark and a wave of his paw.
He could stand on his hind legs and dance to the music of
Nema's fiddle. Day and night he was at Momo's side, in the
house or on the hills, and always lovingly obedient to her least
command, a merry and adoring companion. He understood,
naturally, all her words and even her thoughts, and Momo returned his love in full measure.

For so long Pempa had been one of the family, and the days

and seasons had rolled by as before, that Nema had at last forgotten Dawa's promise of the adventure and fortune he was to bring. Then, when least expected, like the sudden flash and crackle of lightning in a mountain storm, adventure came.

It was one of those days when everything goes wrong. First the logs were green and would not burn; then the fire got so hot that it scorched the millet Momo was trying to dry. Her mother spilled some of the precious grain into the flames and burned her hand in trying to save it. So, although it was very unusual for them not to feel peaceful, they both felt cross and disturbed. Momo was cheered when she heard the silvery tinkle of a mule train, and then the tapping of little hoofs on the stones of the road.

"Yes," she called to her mother from the door, "it is a mule train carrying wool—forty mules and five men and a black dog."

"Then come and watch this stew, while I serve them," said her mother, giving her the big spoon.

The five men stamped into the little house. "Whew!" they said, and took off their thick felt hats, thumped them on the table, and sat down. Each man pulled his tea cup from out of the fold in his robe and waited for it to be filled full of the hot buttered tea. They sucked up the curds and blew on the tea, while they told Momo's mother news of the road and the weather. Their black dog had followed them into the room, and Momo was watching him try to make friends with Pempa when her mother smelled the stew burning.

"Keep on stirring the stew and watch the fire," she said crossly. "Those embers are too hot." Momo obediently pushed more wood into the fire. Then the smoke came up so thick and white all about her, for there is no chimney in a poor Tibetan house, and she was so busy with her stew, that she could see no more until the fire had burned down again, and the stew was cooked. Long before this the men had got up and stamped away, and she had heard the silvery tinkle of the mule bells start up and die away in the distance.

"Where is Pempa?" she asked her mother.

"I don't know, I haven't seen him," she replied. So Momo looked in all the corners of their one-room house, and then went outside to call him.

"Pempa! Pempa-a-a!" He did not come.

Down the single street of their village Momo ran. He must have gone to the woods. She scanned the road that fell with the stream and the mountainside down to the Chumbi valley and saw nothing; with her keen, far-seeing eyes she searched the hillsides on both sides, and saw nothing. Then she threw her head back, her mouth and throat wide open, and called him.

"Pempa-a-a! Pem-pa-a-a!"

Standing quite still, she listened to her voice. It went traveling in waves of sound, clear and full where she stood, fainter as it traveled farther, until it died away at last, and the air was still again. There was no answering joyous bark, no flash of gold among the trees. She tried once more, putting all her strength into the call.

"Pem-pa-a-a-a!"

Up to the very peak of the Jelep La, and down to the swift flowing waters of the Chumbi river that cry would be heard— by Pempa, if not by man. Wherever he ran, however far from home he wandered in the woods, Pempa could always hear her call. He never failed to come bounding to her side, tossing his plumed tail in joy. So Momo waited and waited again, a very long time. He did not come.

She turned and went through the village, looking into every house as she passed. Six men sat playing cards on a sunny upper verandah.

"Oh, Grandfather Tundoop!" she called to the oldest man among them, "have you seen my dog Pempa?" They all looked up smiling from their game, shook their heads, and returned to the cards. Now a great fear began to eat at Momo's heart, and she ran quickly through the rest of the few houses in their village. No one had seen him. A little boy playing by the roadside just above the village finally called down to her.

"Pempa is gone."

"Gone?" cried Momo, rushing up to him. "Where? How?"

The little boy laughed. "One of those men from the mule train carried him off. He tied all his legs together, and stuck wool in his mouth and tied it up to keep him from howling. And even then what a time Pempa was giving him!" The little boy laughed again at the thought.

His words went through Momo's heart like the cold steel of a dagger; she felt the blow, felt her blood dripping slowly, slowly out. Her knees trembled, and her legs felt wobbly under her like melting candles.

"Where have they taken him?" she said through stiff lips, and did not recognize her voice, it was so shrill and thin.

The boy looked wise. "I heard the thief say to the other men, who told him to let it go, 'I am going to carry this demon down to Calcutta, if it fights me every step of the way!'"

"Oh!" Momo gasped. "I must catch them," and started rushing blindly up the path.

"*Catch* them?" the boy echoed. "You can't overtake them

now. They've been gone for hours." But Momo paid him no heed.

A sudden thought made her turn back and run to her home. It would take time, she might have to go far before she caught up with the mule train. If she got very hungry she could not walk so fast. Momo had learned this lesson. Once, when she had gone with herdsmen cousins who were grazing their yaks in the high mountain meadows, she had got separated from the rest, and had wandered a whole day without food. She would never forget that it is not easy to go lightly and quickly over the mountains when the stomach is quite, quite empty.

In her home she slipped a couple of strings of tsampa beads off the hook, and hung them round her throat like necklaces. Her tea cup was already in the pouch of her robe. She filled it with the round bread cakes her mother had been baking; with these she was ready to travel fast and far. Then she looked for her mother, and found her at last, very busy helping to care for the Tundoop baby, who was sick.

"Mother, mother!" she said softly, to catch her attention. But her mother and the baby's mother had eyes only for the sick little one. Momo pulled at her mother's skirts and spoke urgently. "Mother! They took Pempa away. I am going after him." Her mother nodded absently, her mind on the gasping baby, not realizing what she had said. Then Momo sped up the path. As she passed the little boy who had told her of the theft, he looked up and shouted at her:

"Too late! You'll never catch them."

Momo did not even hear him. She did not remember Dawa's words, and his promise of adventure; she did not think how far she might have to go, or how she could snatch back her Pempa from the thief when overtaken. She did not realize that she was leaving her home and her father and mother, and starting out alone to journey in a strange land. Only one thought filled all her mind and heart, and put the strength of a giant into her legs: "Pempa! I must get him back."

Luckily, she could not lose her way. There was only one road —the Great Trade Route; and Momo knew it well from the long talks of the muleteers as they sat drinking tea and recalling the difficulties of their journey. The great stone staircase from Jeyluk to Lingtam, which tried the legs and balance of the mules to the uttermost; the round-cobbled way below Sedon-chen, more slippery than ice when wet; the deep-padded forests leading down to Rongli bazaar, where leeches clung to their legs and sucked blood—all this Momo knew from the lively talk of the muleteers. She had even heard the judgment that a new British officer pronounced upon the Great Trade Route, when he stopped in their tea shop on his way to take up his duties in Gyantse: "That is beyond a doubt the worst road in the world. A road! It isn't even a trail; it's a heap of rocks and the bed of a stream."

As far as the top of the Jelep La pass, Momo knew the way by heart. For in good weather, when her father and his companion, Sakya Tsering, were starting off in the morning, their mail pouches on their backs, Momo often ran along with them to the mountain top, just for the fun of going and of being with her father. So she knew what the Englishman had meant. Much of the way to the top of the pass, the Great Trade Route out of Tibet was under water. It took as the easiest way the path that the little Chumbi river was cutting for itself down the side of the Jelep La mountain.

So now she moved easily and with great speed, wading through the still pools and splashing over stony shallows where the water gurgled and the sunlight made rippling, dancing patterns over the stones. She dodged around great boulders, and sped as if on wings through the forest, up to heights where no trees could grow, and the way was a steep mass of crumbling rock. Up, up, up—until she saw the blue sky above the heap of stones and white prayer banner that marked the top of the pass.

Even in her haste Momo did not forget to pause here for prayer. Gathering a few stones and tossing them upon the cairn about the prayer flag, she made a prayer to the guardian country gods. Then turning, she looked back upon her own country. Range on range the vast mountains of Tibet rose: first the steep wall that hemmed in the Chumbi valley, purpled now in the distance; behind that a sawtooth line of snowy peaks; and directly before her eyes in the far distance, yet seeming to pierce the highest heaven, the glistening white cone of Chomolhari, isolated and perfect.

To Chomolhari, a goddess of great power, Momo made a brief appeal: "O mighty goddess, bring back my Pempa to me! Be gracious! Hear my words!" Then, and not until then, Momo turned her back upon Tibet, and raced along the summit to look down into the neighboring country of Sikkhim.

The road made a series of zigzags, sharply and clearly visible, for not even shrubs grew here on the bald head of the mountain. Momo scanned it all eagerly, quickly. Not a mule, not a man, not a dog, moved up or down the steep slopes. Not even a bird flying gave life to this quiet world. Only the deep blue of the sky all round and over her, the bare rocky mountain, and just under the shadow of the Jelep La, tucked into a hollow, a pair of little lakes, lustrous like black pearls.

"Of course, they could not be so near as this," she told herself to cover her disappointment. And scorning the sidewise line of the switchbacks, made for laden mules, she plunged straight down the face of the mountain, jumping from rock to rock, sliding down the shale, skimming the earth like a bird. While she was still near the top of the mighty Jelep La, she could see far down and away to the end of the world, it seemed. Her eyes passed lightly over the lower ranges of the Himalayas, crowding together in upsurging, jumbled heaps of blue and green. Far, far below these solid hills the earth lay flat, a deep turquoise blue, and shimmering away in the distance till it melted into the paler blue of the sky. As she gazed, Momo could hardly tell where the earth ended and the sky began.

"India!" she murmured in rapture. "Ah! It is indeed the land of the turquoise, even as the muleteers and the holy lama Pakyung have said." And for a moment she forgot her alarm and haste to marvel at the broad and shining world spread out beneath her. She repeated to herself now words that she had never forgotten, read to them from *The Book of the White Lapis Lazuli* by the lama Pakyung while he lay ill in their home:

" 'At the foot of the giant mountains upholding the sky, lakes and flowing streams gather, *so that the plain below the high hills is like unto the turquoise*, being blue and shining even as the world-ravishing gem.' "

There it was before her eyes still just as the holy writer of *The Book of the White Lapis Lazuli* had found it hundreds of years before—a plain blue as the turquoise and luminous like a dream. Now Momo understood the awe that was in the voices of the men of Khamba when they spoke of this land of India. Few of them ever left the hills; they sold off their wool at Kalimpong, made their own purchases there, and returned. India they looked on from afar. And when they saw that it was like the

turquoise they knew it must be a land of great enchantment and of power.

For the turquoise is to all Tibetans a most precious jewel. They love it for its beauty and they believe it has magic power. It is the symbol of power and of wealth, the wealth of this world and the wealth of the soul; and it is the outward sign of sover-eignty. Only officials may wear the long single turquoise earring which is the badge of rank, though all, even the poorest, men as well as women, are never contented or secure until they can wear a fleck of the magic stone, in a nose, or ear, or finger ring. However small it may be, the precious gem will protect them from danger and evil, and will link them to God.

So Momo stood still and gazed with great awe at her first sight of that shimmering land of turquoise. "It is the holy land out of which the great Padma Sambhava came, to teach us of the blessed Buddha," she thought, remembering her mother's teaching. Then suddenly another thought struck her.

"Calcutta is down there! They are taking my Pempa there!" And this thought brought her back to herself and put wings into her feet, so that she floated over the stony way like a cloud. Down into the rhododendron thickets, rounding shoulders, following the curves of the great Jelep La's form, she sped. At last she entered a long canyon, where a wild little stream stormed over boulders, and the daylilies' long leaves, flattened by the frost, made yellow mats, soft to step on. Here she quick-ened her gait. For now she was close to the hamlet of Kapup, where her father certainly, and perhaps the mule train too, would be spending the night.

Though it was still afternoon the canyon was already sunless. High up, as she looked, she could see the snowy peaks still shin-ing in full light, but all around her the cool, damp evening breezes began to rise. She hurried even more and ran down with the wild little stream to Kapup. Four or five flat-roofed little houses, each with its huge round stack of wood beside it, made up the village. Even before she approached, Momo's heart had sunk. There was not a mule in sight; the caravan must have gone on, and therefore she too must follow and at once.

For a moment she paused before the door of the house where Sakya Tsering lived, and where she knew her father was sitting with him by the fire. They would be playing cards and drinking tea there as they did in her own house; and when her father got a lucky hand, he would seize his round felt hat, and thump it up and down upon the table in glee. Oh, how Momo wanted to see him! She would rush in, surprise him: "See, here I am!" And then, when she had told him her story, how she would love to fall upon his breast and cry and cry and cry until there was not a tear left. Standing there before the closed door in the late afternoon light, Momo hesitated. Within, warmth and hot tea and her kind, loving father; outside the light being drained away from a strange world, and she there alone, with such a pain at her heart!

"Just for a moment!" She was moving to the door, lifting her hand to push it open when another thought came. "He will say, 'Pempa is gone, like the snows of last winter, little one. That is sad. But come home with me now and you shall have another dog. Your uncle will bring you one when he comes from Lhasa.'"

Momo nodded her head with bitter remembrance of the long years when her kindly father had fed her upon this thin promise. No, she must not see him. If she did, her search would end here at Kapup, and Pempa be lost forever.

Pempa! Lost! Every moment he was being carried farther

and farther from her, while she stood thinking of herself! Momo turned her back on the door of Sakya's house—and none too soon did she start running down the street. For behind her the door opened and as she ran she heard her father's merry laugh. Only suppose they should come out into the street and see her, call her back, stop her! She did not dare turn her head, nor run so fast as to attract attention; but went ahead steadily with the light, springing kind of half run of the muleteers, wishing herself invisible, until a turn in the road and lift in the hill took her out of sight of Kapup. Then she breathed more freely.

Now looking behind her she saw the snow peaks still gleaming in bright sunlight; but down in this valley evening would soon come, and then the dark, in which she could not find the path. Gnatong, she knew, was not far from Kapup. Perhaps there the thieving muleteers were resting for the night. Some-time, somewhere, they would halt, remove the packs from their weary mules, and let them feed and drink and rest. Oh, if only she could come upon them now, before they started another day's march! She hastened on more quickly.

This was a splendid great wide path to travel over. It lifted her up along the side of the Nim La, an unforested mountain at whose base the long body of Bidang Lake stretched deep gray in this sunless world. Shaggy black yaks bathed in the waters. As she went steadily climbing upward, Momo repeated to her-self what she knew of the road, to keep up her courage.

"That is the Bidang Lake, and this mountain the Nim La. Then comes the open land where once the white-faced English and our own men fought. And when we stopped fighting, we let them send an officer to sit in Gyantse and direct the mails. So father says. Then after this plain comes the Taku La—but these two are little peaks, not like the mighty Jelep, and quickly passed. Then comes the town of Gnatong, and there, perhaps *there*, I shall find my Pempa."

With this thought to cheer her she ran down the side of the Nim La, crossed the rolling upland where once her own people had fought the British, and moved lightly up the side of the Taku La, through rhododendron thickets, then over a jumble of black rock, up to the heap of rocks and the prayer flag that marked its peak. Here again Momo tossed a stone upon the cairn, and murmured a prayer. Then she looked down and was disappointed not to see the roofs of Gnatong below her.

Instead, she was looking down into a narrow valley, with the long shoulder of another hill hiding Gnatong from her. And every moment the light was fading. Soon it would be quite dark. Momo drew a deep breath, and not giving herself time to feel weariness or discouragement, ran down to the valley and up the side of this unwelcome hill. And there from its summit she saw the straggling houses of Gnatong, set in a swampy bowl. It was a dreary, cheerless place, and Momo shivered as she strained her eyes to find, through the graying light, the mule train she was following.

Every house was still visible, and each might have been empty. Not a creature moved in the hamlet; not a cheery mule bell tinkled; no lights shone through half-open doors. This might have been a ghost town. And as she looked and bit her lip to keep back the tears, Momo suddenly remembered the gossip she had heard in the tea shop at home about this village of Gnatong.

It was a place of violence; of fights and murder and the restless spirits of the dead. Here Tibetans with an uncontrollable enmity fled to fight and kill or be killed—taking themselves and their evil passions out of Tibet, not to pollute their holy land with the great sin of murder, nor to burden their people with the angry spirits of the dead. Evil was drawn to the place as the sun drew up rain from the earth. The muleteers spoke sometimes of a band of robbers that had once come up out of Nepal and made their hiding place in the bare hills above Gnatong; from there they swooped down upon the ascending mule trains to rob and kill, until at last a strong troop of Indian soldiers had come and after a desperate battle had captured the robbers.

So great and general was the horror of the place that only rough men of Bhutan, who feared neither gods nor demons, would live there. Her father, she remembered, had come home one night with a tale of the new officer of the posts and the telegraph line in Tibet. The government of India had put up a new, strongly built house for this official of theirs; one room was his office, the rest was his home. And when the man and his wife and five children arrived, they were delighted with the cool air of the hills, and their fine, new home. Their joy lasted one day only. For after the first night, the wife had gathered up her brood of children and fled back to their old home in Bengal, without even waiting for their clothes to be packed and carried back with her to the plains.

And the man, who could not leave his work, locked himself into his house at sunset, Nema had said, and prayed. Every day he sent letters and wires begging for a transfer from this post— anywhere in India, he implored—*anywhere*, out of this accursed spot. Nema and the muleteers and Sakya had laughed at his funny little figure, and his shivering terror. But her mother, who was always sympathetic, had said in her gentle way, "Poor man! Feel pity for him. You yourselves would not like to live there."

They admitted it. No mule train stopped there, Momo now remembered, except in the direst need, but pressed on to Kapup, only four miles away. And here she was alone in the place at nightfall without even the shelter of a roof over her head! Momo was as brave as anyone to face the dangers of this world—but ghosts and all the company of evil spirits—these indeed she feared. She had never guessed how deeply she feared them until now, when she stood alone in the gray, chill air of this unholy place. The hair bristled on her scalp, her skin crawled and quivered, shivers ran up and down her spine and her knees knocked together so that she could hardly stand.

"Mother! Mother!" she wailed aloud. If only she were there, Momo would have clung to her, catching strength and courage from her. Her prayers and her faith she knew would save them from any evil. For her mother had grown up as a serving maid in the household of a wealthy Hindu wool merchant in Rinchengong. In this pious household she had been taught that there is only one God, whom different men call by different names; that He alone is real, and not evil. And therefore Momo's mother always prayed with great faith to the One Lord of the universe, and she had no fear of the demons, evil spirits, and ghosts whom, in spite of the teachings of the Lord Buddha, the people of Tibet still feared. She wanted Momo too to live in faith, and unafraid.

But from her father Momo had learned some fear. To Nema the Lord Buddha was good, no doubt, but very far away, beyond all sight or knowing. And the powers of evil—these were very close and terrible to Nema. He spent his days battling against them. There were the vast mountains, goddesses of great power; the guardian country gods; the deities of place, who dwelt in rocks, trees, or springs—spiteful creatures who in ill temper love to vex mankind; the earth demons; the bold demons of the sky, and all the devils, and ghosts of the spirits of the dead. Some of these spirits were kind to man, but most were not.

Brave as he was, Nema feared them. He *saw* them, and he felt their power. Day after day, as he struggled over the top of the Jelep La pass, he fought against them. He watched the evil weather demon come riding up from the east and the south in a wild black thundercloud, bringing torrents of rain or hail to destroy their small hill crops of maize. In the late summer months as he climbed to the top of the Jelep La he was so close to the sky that he seemed almost to be in the battlefield, and a helpless part of the warfare raging there. For then the white demons of the north, who had been sleeping through the rainy season, rose and met the dark demons of the south, and the two strove for mastery. In these great cloud battles the demons of the north would finally win and drive away for another winter the black rain clouds.

Then for a time Nema would rejoice in the gentle demons of the sky. They came streaming down from the north, led by Old Father Khen-pa, the master of the sky. With joy Nema watched Old Father Khen-pa, dressed in white robes, with snow-white hair, and carrying a crystal wand, come riding on the white dog of the sky. But even Old Father Khen-pa was not always kind. The snow and ice he brought were the greatest dangers of all the year for Nema. Three times had he not seen his companion mail carrier swallowed up before his very eyes, lost forever in the wild snowstorms that swept over the head of the Jelep La? When danger was so near and terrible that any step might plunge him into death, how indeed could Nema pray to a faraway spirit? He needed strong and immediate support. Therefore his body was strung round with little charm boxes, made powerful by an inset spot of turquoise and by the written prayers within, blessed by the lamas. And as he toiled up the mountainside, Nema snapped his fingers to keep off the evil spirits, and his lips moved constantly in prayer.

All this Momo knew. All these fears and more crowded into her mind as she stood alone in the last uncertain light, and looked down on the village of Gnatong. The road led down and through it, and over the rocky hill beyond. That way Pempa had gone, and unless she were to give up and go home, that way she too must go. Choking back her sobs, with her hand on the charm she wore round her neck, and a prayer on her lips, she rushed down the hill like a whirlwind, and passed through the village without even so much as making a dog come out to bark. So she started up the rocky hill.

But now the light was quite gone. No stars shone in a black and clouded sky, and she could not see the path. Still she pushed on, knowing that she must get beyond this evil hill before she stopped to rest. Stumbling, falling against stones, she felt the cold, damp air rise out of the swamp and strike her feverish skin. A white mist came blowing along with it, moving toward her, enveloping her, wrapping her round like clammy, cold fingers, so that she was swallowed in its chill. Then she heard a low sighing sound that came out of the very earth, and she shuddered from head to foot. She felt that something, *something*, was here. It was all about her, and it was something very strange.

"Ai! Ai!" she wailed. For now she remembered. This, the very earth under her, was the burial ground of the British soldiers who had fallen in that battle long ago with her own

people. And of all the ghosts, these, the foreign dead, were the most evil. Black and malignant devils, they were never to be appeased but by the sacrifice of a pig. She shrieked in terror.

"*Ai! Ai-i!*" She shrieked again when her cry came back to her in echoes.

Stumbling, falling and rising, she plunged on. Her heart and her lungs were bursting, her throat was taut and aching so that she could hardly gasp her prayers aloud.

"Oh Tara, Mother of mercy, save me! You, who are the best of gods, do not abandon me! Protect me on all sides as by a thick tent! Save me, Tara, save me!"

Now out of that chill white mist, and above the deep sighing that came up out of the earth, came still another sound. It was a breathing, deep and very close to her. Momo stood still, shaking like a leaf. Something cold and damp touched her hot skin.

"*Ai—Ai! Ai-i-i!*" Momo screamed again and again. With a great effort, she forced her leaden legs to move—stumbled—and rolled down through the darkness. She felt herself falling, falling—then everything was black and blank, and she felt no more.

III. THE GIANT STAIRCASE AND THE FOREST

It was quite light when Momo opened her eyes. For a moment she felt confused.

"Where am I? What is this?" she thought, surprised not to see around her the walls of her snug little home. Then she moved, her head throbbed, and at once all that happened the day before came flooding back into her mind. She jumped up and looked anxiously about.

She was lying in a grassy spot on the edge of the swamp of Gnatong; and all about her quiet black yaks were grazing. One came up to her as she stood and breathed down her neck, with a gentle curiosity. Momo laughed aloud, remembering her terror of the night, and turning, she playfully pummeled the great beast.

"O black and shaggy one!" she cried. "Never again play such tricks on the poor night-bound traveler!" She was in high spirits to see the sky clear, and tiny clouds high overhead turning pink from the light of the rising sun. Except for a headache from a bump she had got in falling, she was unhurt, and refreshed by her night's sleep; and more determined than the day before to overtake the muleteer who had stolen her dog and make him return Pempa to her.

She said her prayers as she stood watching the light in the east grow every moment brighter and more warm, until the great gold sun rose over the mountain top, and made all the dewy grass around her glisten like jewels. Her heart swelled; in this glow she felt warm and confident.

"O Precious Jewel in the Lotus! O blessed Tara! Bring me to Pempa, and carry us both in safety to our home!" she finished. And then, having said her prayers, she felt ravenously hungry; so she pulled out some of the bread from her blouse, and munched it as she climbed back to the Great Trade Route. Behind her now was the British burial ground that had given her such terror the night before, and before her the crest of the hill she had tried in vain to climb in the darkness of the night.

Now she reached it quickly, and looked down upon a wide view of open downs and rolling slopes. Above and through a silver veil the sun was shining, and drawing up to itself a light mist that clung to these slopes; and in the gray but luminous light on the downs, the frost-reddened leaves and late autumn flowers made a carpet wonderfully bright.

Momo ran lightly along this easy bit of ups and downs. Once she paused to see how blossoming gentians turned a whole rocky slope into one great sapphire. But there were so many flowers,

all so beautiful and gay! Her quick eyes took them all in with joy, as she ran.

The morning was still early when she looked down from a height and saw her pathway go twisting like a corkscrew around the steep hill; and dotted along these curves were a few houses —the village of Lingtu. Here, as in every hill village, Momo knew, the wife of the *dak* runner (mail carrier) would keep, just as her own mother did, a little tea house for the travelers. Which one was it, she wondered? "Will she give me some tea?" she asked herself this anxiously, for she felt she could run all day like Pempa himself if only she had some nourishing hot tea to start the day—and without it she was already feeling empty.

In no time she had reached the first house of the village, and stood peeping in the open door. It was a house like her own—one room, with a connecting storeroom, the walls and roof gleaming black from the oil and smoke of many years. As it had neither windows nor chimney, the place was full of billowing smoke. Momo breathed in the air happily. How she loved the smell of burning wood fires! She made out the forms of two women working at the earthen stove. One was kneading great flat bread cakes, shaping them over the bottom of a pot and setting them in a huge round pan to bake. The other was very busy feeding the fire, dipping water up into pots that stood on the stove, and making tea. When Momo saw the size of the two copper teapots that stood steeping in the warmth at the back of the stove, she knew this was the tea shop, and went inside.

"Have you seen a mule train of forty mules and five men, and two dogs, one yellow and one black?" she asked.

Both women looked up from the stove. The older one, who was making a pot of tea, said, "They passed this way yesterday. I did not notice the dogs."

"But I did," cried a little girl Momo's age, coming around the corner of the stove. "The yellow one was tied by a rope, and tried to bite the man who led him. He had to throw food to the dog."

"That was Pempa, my dog," said Momo. "The man stole him out of my house, and I am going to get him back."

Both women left their work at the stove, and came to where Momo stood by the door.

"Who are you?" asked the older woman, the mother of the household.

"I am Momo, and I live near the top of the Jelep La pass. My father is the dak runner who carries the mails from our village of Longram to Kapup, and sleeps there the night, and then next day returns to Longram. Send word to him, please, by the mail carriers who go on from here, that I am well, and will come home when I have got my Pempa back."

"The men of that mule train are on their way down to the plains, leaving their mules in Kalimpong till they return," she said. "You cannot go there. Go home, little Momo, and your father will get you another dog."

Momo shook her head obstinately. "I don't want another dog. Besides, there is no other like Pempa. He is of the household of our priestly ruler, the Great Gem of Majesty, the Dalai Lama himself—that is why he is stolen."

The little girl still staring, said, "He is a fine one, mother—all red-gold, and his hair hangs over his eyes like the silken covering of a prayer banner."

"Yes, it does indeed," said Momo proudly.

Her mother shook her head again and said to Momo, "But child, you don't understand. You will walk for days up the mountains and then down into the valleys, up and down, up and down, and every time the valleys will be hotter and the air more steaming. You will come to a land where no one will understand what you say. And then you will come to a very large town, with a huge bazaar. That is Kalimpong. And from near there a great thing called a *te-rain* takes all the wool and the people who want to go down to the plains of India; and it rushes down the hills as fast as the waters in spring when the snow is melting. But no one can set foot upon that *te-rain* without the paying of much money. And you have no money."

But Momo only said obstinately, "I am going to get my dog."

The woman sighed and shook her head again. Then she said, "Well, go and see that it is as I have said. But first sit down and let me give you a cup of hot tea; for your father's and your mother's sake I will feed their child."

So Momo sat down very gladly, and pulled her tea cup out of her blouse. The woman filled it three times with hot buttered tea. And the younger woman stopped kneading and molding bread cakes long enough to give her first one, then a second one, of the golden hot breads. Oh, how good it tasted, the crisp fresh bread, and this comforting hot tea! Momo drank it slowly, partly in politeness, partly to keep that delicious warming taste as long as possible. The little girl of the house sat at the table opposite her, and stared.

When she had taken the last bite of the bread and the last swallow of tea, Momo jumped to her feet, and cried, "Thank you, thank you. May you be rich! May no sickness come to you!" And to the little girl she added, "I'll stop again on my way home, and show you the tricks my Pempa can do." And she fled down the winding corkscrew, and out of sight.

Now the mountain was so sheer a drop that even the zigzag

twists of the switchbacks were almost vertical. And here the road had once been laid with giant stones, like a great staircase. Some had been displaced by the rush of monsoon rains, some had rolled quite away, and the holes thus left made the going much harder for the patient, burdened mules, especially on their downward passage. Many were the tales the muleteers told of slips and falls, and the losing of wool packs, down this difficult descent.

"*This,*" said Momo to herself, as if greeting an old friend, "is the giant staircase." And hearing the sweet jangle of oncoming mule bells behind her she stood aside to watch the mules carry their heavy packs down this headlong drop—shifting their burden skillfully, placing each little hoof with sure instinct so as not to slip or stumble. The men kept a careful eye on their mules, and themselves jumped lightly from one to another of the great stone treads of the staircase. They smiled at Momo, showing their white teeth, as they passed.

"But," Momo told herself, "I have no time to let the mule trains pass me by!" And in her pliant red felt boots she leaped nimbly down the mountain, leaving the giant staircase to the wool trains, but keeping close beside it, lest she lose her way.

Rhododendron forests covered this steep slope. In the bright morning light she looked down over these forests of burnished leaves, beyond the lower ranges of the Himalayas, and saw again far below that land of the turquoise plain, where shining rivers gleamed like silver snakes through the blue haze.

"*Lah-se!*" she murmured to herself. "It is a wondrous place, that land of India."

Close about her too the forest became from moment to moment more beautiful. The ground she trod was carpeted with late blooming flowers, blue gentians, pink gloxinia, and yellow mimulus, and already the winter ground-covers of wintergreen and ground pine were in red berry. These she knew, for there could be no more beautiful flowers in all the world than in her own home, and the Chumbi valley. But she looked in awe at the trees, hung with moss. Green or brown mosses clothed their trunks like close-fitting velvet sheaths, and a long gray trailing kind hung like great cobwebs from the branches, swaying lightly in the breeze.

Coming to a clearing in the forest, she looked down on a half-dozen little houses, flat-roofed, and like her own, dotted with heavy stones to keep the furious winter winds from lifting them and sending them flying through the air.

"Jeyluk!" she said to herself—and so indeed it was. Here Momo had no idea of stopping, and only smiled in passing at a young woman, with bright pink cheeks and a cheery smile, who stood lounging in the sunshine at her doorway.

"Ho, little girl!" she called. "Are you traveling the Great Trade Route? Stop and have a cup of tea with me."

So Momo turned back and entered the tea house.

"Who are you?" asked the pretty young woman.

"I am Momo and I live near the top of the Jelep La pass. My father carries the mails, and my mother keeps a tea shop in Longram. And I go to get back my dog Pempa, that was stolen from me yesterday by some muleteers. A golden Lhasa terrier —did you see him?" she finished eagerly.

The young woman stopped swirling the tea about in the big copper teapot she held. She stared at Momo, and asked, "You go alone? Do your mother and father know?"

Momo wriggled. "I told my mother I was going to get Pempa back," she said. "And she just nodded, and went on looking at the little sick Tundoop baby."

The young woman sat down across the table from Momo, and poured them each a cup of tea. She blew thoughtfully on the steaming brew, and watched the curling vapor. Then she said, "Go back, Momo. That mule train is traveling at forced marches; you cannot overtake them now. I do not think your mother meant you to go so far alone. She must be full of fear and sorrow now. And your father also."

Momo stared at her in distress. She had not thought of that. Suddenly—"Ah!" she said, remembering the words of Dawa, on that night when Pempa was named. She replied confidently:

"They will not feel fear or sorrow. This journey of mine is written in the stars and set down on my horoscope. Dawa the astrologer foretold it on the night when Pempa first came to us."

Now it was the tea-shop woman's turn to stare. "What?" she said. "It is written in the stars?"

Momo nodded, swelling with importance. "It is indeed," she said. "We go to great adventure, Pempa and I, and he, the red-gold Lhasa terrier from the household of the Great Gem of Majesty, will bring fortune to us all. Thus it is written." She swallowed down the last of her tea, and was about to push the tea cup back in her blouse, when the young woman spoke.

"Take one more cup, then, O fortunate Momo." She poured it full, and Momo drank it down more quickly, and rising said, "My father and my mother will remember the words of Dawa, and will have no fear. I think," she added, remembering how quickly her prayers at Kargayu were answered, "that we are under the special blessing of the Enlightened One."

The woman nodded. "That must be so," she observed, "from the words of the horoscope. I will send word along by my husband to the other dak runners, to say that you are on the way to the fulfillment of the prophecy, and for them to be at peace."

"Oh, thank you! May all good befall you!" cried Momo. "And when I return you'll see Pempa for yourself. Then you'll see yourself that he is truly of the household of our blessed ruler the Dalai Lama."

And once again she stepped out into the sunlight and shot down the mountain like an arrow. The staircase here was worse than ever, the stones with which it was laid being small and slippery. Momo paused to watch with great sympathy one line of mules slip painfully over the edges of these rounded cobbles, stumble, catch themselves before falling headlong, recover their balance, and go plunging down, down, down. Their great packs of fuzzy gray wool slipped and wobbled and looked as if at any moment they might go sliding right over the mules' heads to roll and fall down into the distant valley. Yet they went patiently, steadily along, needing no prompting from the alert muleteers.

"Ha!" Momo chided herself. "Have you nothing to do but to stand all day watching the red tassels of the mule trains, and listening to the music of their bells?"

And she leaped again down the mountain, and was soon far from the jangle of bells and the clatter of hoofs, deep in the stillness of the forest. This was a place of dim enchantment. Light, high mists had drifted over the sun, and mingled with the heavier mist of lacy moss that trailed from the upper branches. Now and then a ray of sunshine filtered through this silver mist, and fell at Momo's feet like a broad arrow, leading her on and down. But no sounds—not even the cry of a bird, nor the rush of water—disturbed the quiet dreaming peace of this forest. Even the roadway here was not stone, but soft earth, over which her feet padded silently.

No other earth was visible, but everywhere covered with

grasses, flowers, trailing green ground covers. And the trees, great majestic beeches and deodars, were hung along the whole of their height with flowering clusters of orchids, pink and yellow and creamy white. Momo looked at them with quick interest. She had heard of these beautiful blooms that live on the tree trunks and make flower gardens in the air. These orchids, and the trails of silvery tree moss, were the first signs to Momo that she had dropped below the high levels of the Tibetan mountains—these, and a certain softening of the air.

Momo lifted her face to the breezes and breathed in deeply, wonderingly. The air in her own homeland was thin and clear, and very often of terrible coldness. But always it was light and so buoyant that, as the muleteers laughingly told her mother when they returned from the lower valleys up into their own land, they could eat the air and draw strength from it. But the breeze now lightly stirring in this forest was—Momo searched for a way of explaining it to herself—*soft*. It was also damper than the dry air of Tibet, as she had proof immediately, when the skies quickly got gray and grayer, and the mists turned into rain that fell with a steady pattering sound upon the forest.

When therefore Momo looked down upon a clearing and saw a clump of barrow-shaped roofs of plaited bamboo around a flagged square, she saw them through the silvery screen of driving rain. Yet even so she knew this village too from the muleteers' descriptions, and said to herself, "Sedonchen!" There were no people in the square or standing in the doorways and Momo passed quickly through this village, and went on skipping and slipping along the steep stairlike way.

The rain fell harder and harder, making a steady drumming noise as it hit the earth. The only other sound that Momo heard was the roar, muffled by the rain and the distance, of the rapid

Rungi river, to whose stream bed she was dropping. All the views of the high snowy mountains, the blue lower Himalayas and the turquoise plain were gone, and she was closed in on all sides by a silver sheet of falling rain. It dripped through her hair, got in her eyes, and washed her face and hands. But Momo pushed back her hair, shook the rain out of her eyes, and went steadily on down.

"Down, down!" she said to herself, "everything is going down—the rain, the road, the mountain, and I. But I go to find Pempa and bring him back!" This thought put courage and cheer into her heart, and she kept repeating the words to herself.

Nevertheless her thick wool dress got heavier and heavier from the rain it absorbed. Her felt boots too were heavy and soaking wet. And when she came out into a clearing in the fork of two hills, she thought how good it would be to sit a moment before a fire and drink a cup of tea.

"This is Lingtam," she said to herself, and she looked about to find the tea shop. Unlike most hill villages, Lingtam was not a cheerful or pretty place even in sunshine, and now, when the rain made the open clearing a muddy runway, it was very ugly. The few houses were worn and dilapidated, with sagging bamboo roofs, and everything looked dismal and dirty. But Momo was longing so for the comfort of hot tea and a fire that she went squashing through the mud to the largest house, where a line of mules huddling together showed her that this was the tea shop and that muleteers were resting there. She went and stood in the doorway, peering into the smoky room.

Inside it was so dark that for a moment she could see nothing; but all the air about the place was steeped in the smells of disgusting filth and rancid butter. Here, Momo felt, the tea would not be good; yet she was so weary, so discouraged by the heavy rain, that she would have taken any kind of tea, if only it were hot and made nourishing with butter and salt. But the voice of the woman who was talking there was both harsh and angry. Every other word was an oath. So Momo stood in the door, still pausing, uncertain whether or not to enter and ask for tea. Two pigs decided for her.

For suddenly the dark and smoky room was in an uproar. What a screaming and squealing, and above it the roar of the muleteers' laughter and the violent cursing of the tea-shop woman! Two half-grown pigs nearly knocked Momo over as they came running out, closely followed by the tea-shop woman, who was swearing at them in her ugly voice and beating them with a thick stick.

"Out of the house, you devils and souls of beggars reborn in a pig's body! By my father's and my mother's flesh! You have all but killed me and drowned me in the scalding tea. The waste of good tea and the costly butter too! Out, or by the Three Rarest Ones, I'll cut your throats and let you bleed to death!" She beat violently as she spoke. Momo gave a little scream as the stick came near her, and jumped aside.

"Who are you and what are you doing here?" the woman snapped, seeing her for the first time.

"I am Momo. O keeper of the open house! Gain merit by cheering the weary with the gift of the warming tea," Momo answered. She pulled the tea cup out of her blouse and rather doubtfully, looking into the angry wrinkled face of the old crone, held it out in the traditional gesture of one begging alms.

But the tea-shop woman was in no mood for charity. She was still furious and in pain from the burn of the scalding tea, which Momo could see had been overturned down the length of her wool robe. So she raised her stick at Momo and snarled.

"May I die before sunset! This is an ill day. First the devils of pigs knock me down and burn me with the loss of a full pot of the costly drink. Then this beggar and brat of a beggar comes whining for a cup of tea." Her voice rose to a scream.

"Out of my house!"

Momo fled before her, down the sagging steps, across the muddy flat, onto the Great Trade Route, and away around the curve of the hill and out of sight. She went like the wind, never stopping until the evil-smelling house and the violent woman were well behind her. Then she drew a deep breath and lifted her face to the rain. After that horrible house even its chill soaking, and the steady drumming noise it made, seemed pleasant and peaceful. So she detached one of the tsampa beads from her necklace and sucked it as she slipped down the path. She observed with a mountaineer's eye every detail of the country she was passing through.

The giant staircase had ended at Lingtam; and even through the heavy rain she could see that these hills were different from the high mountains of her home, and also from that dim, enchanted forest of orchids and tree moss. Here the hills were more open, separated by wider valleys. Sometimes, spiraling round a mountainous flank, she could look through a clearing in the rain clouds and see the turbulent Rungi, tearing down the hills in its mad career to the plains. The roar of the river, swollen now by the rains, came up to her in a steady booming thunder that got louder and louder the nearer she dropped to its level.

All round her was the roar and the rush of falling water. From every cleft in the hills a stream came leaping, crossing the road over which she passed, to fall again down the face of the mountain, and join the Rungi. Great waterfalls across the valley she saw, falling in two and even three sheer drops, from the top of the mountain to its foot. The hills were a vivid green, with flowering trees ablaze with crimson and yellow bloom. And round and round the hills the road curled, making one, two, three spirals, each one carrying Momo nearer to the river bottom. When the road became a wide cobbled way, plunging down to a clearing, Momo wiped the rain out of her eyes and looked and listened. For this must be the cobbled way that the muleteers said led to Rongli.

Next in size and importance to Kalimpong, they said, was this bazaar town of Rongli, on a slope above the Rungi river, and a favorite halting place for the wool caravans. Here Momo was sure to get news of the thieves and of Pempa. She forgot her fatigue in her eagerness, and ran down to where bamboo stalls lined the roadway.

It was market day and the place was crowded with people, all like herself moving about with no protection from, and paying no attention to, the rain that fell with soaking persistence. Only here and there an Indian trader, his white *dhoti* tucked up to his knees, walked under a huge black umbrella; and a few hill men had made themselves a peaked cap of two banana leaves. Otherwise the people crowding the stalls stood in the wet and looked in at the open booths, where the merchants sat cross-legged among their wares.

As Momo passed down the street and looked in at the stalls, she forgot her quest for a moment in wondering at the treasures spread out before the eyes of the throng. Such heaps of silver bracelets and anklets, and such clothes! Men and women both stood looking at the cotton cloth for women's *saris,* piled bolt on bolt up to the very ceiling of the shops. How pretty, the hues of rose and blue and green, and the patterns! And how graceful these saris, long pieces of straight cloth, draped round and round the body, to fall in fanplaits at the women's bare feet. Rain-soaked as they were, or half hidden under shawls, these hill women looked beautiful and dainty.

"Like butterflies," Momo thought to herself, admiringly. Then glancing down at her own dark wool and shapeless robe, she thought, "And I am like an old black crow."

The children's clothes were even more enchanting. Whole stalls were full of holiday dress for children, in shining satin, red and blue and yellow. Tiny frocks for little girls, an adored son's first short trousers, they swung on gently curving lines across the shop, the better to tempt doting parents.

And the food! Tibet is a hard, wintry land, where with great difficulty her people grow a few grains and turnips. Momo had never seen or even imagined such kinds and quantities of vegetables and fruits as filled the low round baskets to overflowing. Here were the round oranges and yellow bananas the muleteers spoke of. And the heaps of red apples—how much bigger they were than the little knobby ones that grew in the Chumbi valley! Momo stood entranced before the beauty of silvery squash and yellow gourds, and heaps of green spinach, and little red peppers. Even the dried foods, how many and how plentiful! There were stalls selling nothing else—a dozen different kinds of rice, red and yellow dal, and heaps of dried yellow corn. Others sold nothing but spice—ginger and clove and cardamom. The very air was sweet about the spice merchants.

When she had walked down the length of the bazaar, staring at every kind of marvel laid out for men to buy, then and not until then, Momo observed the faces of people around her. They too were, she saw, different from any she had seen before. She could not understand their words. Some she knew by sight to be men of Bhutan, from their heavy, flat-featured faces and huge build. Then there were the Lepchas, a gentle folk, with delicate, flower-like features, dreamy and lovely to look upon. Men and women of Nepal too were there, golden-skinned and graceful, with bright glancing black eyes. A few Chinese, moving with rhythmic ease in their trousers and loose coats, had faces of a pale oval, and drooping black mustaches. And sitting in the stalls were the merchants from India—big, soft men of Bengal or the Punjab, with abundant black hair and huge black eyes. They sat cross-legged among their clothes or their copper and brass utensils, and waited quietly for buyers.

One shop had been so closely crowded about with children that Momo had not been able to see what was there. Now when the group broke up, and some of the children moved away, Momo saw a man sitting on the floor with two great black kettles before him. He was cooking sweetmeats, and sat stirring the boiling honey, paying no attention to the flies and the children swarming about him. Momo slipped into the gap, sniffing with delight the sweet smell of the honey, watching with a fascinated gaze while the sweetmeat-man lifted a great spoon of the thick, amber-colored sweet, twirled it into a circle, and laid it to take shape on the constantly growing heap of golden circlets before him.

Such treasures of sweetness Momo had heard of. Her mother had eaten them in the home of her Indian master as a girl; the wealthy folk of Tibet also eat candied sweets as well as cakes and dumplings. But never had Momo laid eyes on these golden *jalebis*, never had she smelled anything so delicious as this boiling honey. She moved up closer and closer, till she was in the front rank, and a sudden push from the back threw her directly under the man's gaze. He looked at her questioningly. She shook her head sadly, as she had no money, and asked, "Have you seen a mule train of forty mules and five men, and a red-gold Lhasa terrier?"

The man said something in a language she did not understand, and smiled. All the children stared at Momo, and one among them, a ragged dirty-faced boy, began making fun of her. He mimicked her speech, made faces at her, and pointed jeeringly at her long woolen robe. The children laughed. Encouraged, he poked more fun at her in a tongue Momo did not know, making the children laugh loud and long with each sally.

The hot blood rushed to Momo's cheeks, and she got very angry. She stamped her foot at the boy, and shouted at him in Tibetan, "What rudeness! Only a pig and the son of a pig and the reborn soul of a pig would be so disobedient to the laws of politeness to the stranger!" The children about her did not understand a word of what she said, but they laughed and laughed at her, the ragged boy imitating in a mocking way her words and gestures. Momo gave him a furious glance, then suddenly remembered her quest.

"Pempa! What am I doing, standing here to make myself a mockery to these children while you are being carried every moment farther from me? And falling into great danger, too!" She felt very penitent, and stood quite still, with bowed head. For by nature Momo was hot-tempered, and her patient mother taught her, when she felt the waves of anger rising in her, always to stop and pray. So now Momo murmured to herself, "O Blessed One, give me enlightenment. Remove far from me the dark sin of anger, and ever keep me close to Thee." Then turning, with no further notice of the children, she made her way through the crowd, and started down the cobbled way.

Behind her a furious outcry started up, a man's voice, screaming with rage, and the high, shrill answering screams of a boy, her ragged tormentor. Glancing back, Momo saw that one of the merchants had leaped down from his booth, and was hanging on to the boy, beating him over the head. All the people standing round and the children too, took up the quarrel, shouting and screaming. What a fight! Momo quickened her steps to a run, eager to escape into the peace of the forest. But the noise and the people seemed to follow her. Again she looked behind her. They *were* following her, chasing her. The teasing boy was pointing at her, the merchant was beckoning to her and, quite clearly, was shouting at her to stop. That cry was taken up all round the bazaar.

"Stop! Stop!"

Momo ran. They ran. She doubled and twisted through the people like a fish gliding through water; still the merchant and the boy were at her heels, and the crowd at theirs. For now they were all after her, like a swarm of angry hornets. Why? What was wrong? Momo had no idea what she had done, but something certainly had turned that whole part of the bazaar behind her furiously against her. Everyone joined in the chase. They were running her down like a pack of angry dogs. Momo was first bewildered, then terrified. What did they want? What were they going to do to her?

She strained to draw her breath in short, agonized pants, through a throat stiff with fright. And in her fear she lost her cunning, and went plunging straight on, headlong into the press of people before her. These, surprised by the general uproar and the crowds sweeping toward them, all began to look up curiously; they asked questions, and soon shouted themselves. The yelling echoed and re-echoed in the narrow river canyon, drowning even the roar of the Rungi river. In her fright Momo could not see where she was going, but ran. Bang! She crashed into a burly man who was just coming out of a shop, and with such force that he knocked her flat.

"Out of my way, you careless brat!" he said angrily, and went on without a glance of curiosity at the crowd, or concern to see if she were hurt. But his words were music to Momo, for he spoke her own Tibetan tongue. She scrambled quickly to her feet.

"Oh stop! Stop!" she shrieked. "O man of Tibet! Help me! Help! Help!"

But he was already out of sight, lost in the crowd. She stood alone in the foreign bazaar, and in that moment's pause was overtaken. The merchant and her tormentor, the ragged boy, caught her, laid heavy hands on her.

"What is the matter? What have I done?" she asked, trembling, looking up at the merchant, whose face was convulsed with rage. He seized her arm and began beating her over the head, for answer. Momo screamed with pain.

"Hai! H-a-i!" Then in a fury she turned to fight. Her own nature and her mother's gentle training in their Buddhist faith gave Momo a horror of violence, but she was no coward, and when angered and set upon unjustly, she could hold her own. Trapped now, held in by the press of hostile people against her two enemies, Momo stood like a panther at bay and fought. She kicked, she bit the boy's finger to the bone, so that he howled and dropped his grip on her. She clawed the merchant, and drew long nail scratches down his cheek. She writhed and twisted out of their grasp.

But what could one child do among so many? The crowd held her fast within its angry circle. The merchant, more furious than before, bound her hands, and helped by the entire crowd began to drag her up the hill.

IV. CAPTURED BY THE WOMAN AT RHENOK

A boy stopped them—a boy not more than twelve years old, who worked his way through the crowd till he stood directly in front of the merchant and Momo. "Ho, Balaram Bose!" he said. "You look as angry as a red tiger devil. What has the girl done?"

The merchant, still shaking with rage, said, "Done! Stolen, in the one second that my back was turned, all the money that lay in my change box before me!" He shook Momo like a rag and started again to drag her forward, pushing the boy aside. But the boy stood firm, and spoke to Momo, and to her joy in her own tongue.

"O daughter of the mountains!" he said. "This merchant

says that you have stolen the whole of his day's takings—all the money that lay in his change box."

"What a lie!" she replied hotly. "I never—"

The boy interrupted her.

"Ho, merchant! Look to your money!" he cried, excitedly, pointing into the crowd. "Catch the real thief—see, where he glides like a snake through the people to make his escape."

As he spoke, the boy leaped through the thick mass of people, and laid hands upon a lad who, taking advantage of the distraction, was quietly gliding away from the bazaar. But the thief slipped out of his hands like a pea out of its pod, leaving only his shirt in the boy's hands.

"Hold him! Stop the thief!" he cried again. The bazaar was in an uproar.

"Stop the thief!"

"There he goes!"

"Where?"

"Here?"

"No, there—catch him!"

"It is Tulsi—Tulsi the beggar! Catch him, stop him!"

"Tulsi! Here he is!"

And there indeed he was, caught and held fast by no less than five men, and brought, still wriggling and trying to escape, before the merchant, who all the while, not to be done out of a scapegoat, had stood holding fast to Momo and watching the turmoil. With great satisfaction Momo observed that she was face to face with the ragged boy who had started to tease her.

"Hah!" she said in contempt. "So you are the thief!"

The merchant dropped his hold on her and made a dive for the ragged boy. "Thief!" he shouted. "Give back that money!"

And he started beating and searching the boy, with the crowd obligingly helping him.

The Tibetan boy pulled Momo, who was now quite forgotten, out of the crush of people and untied her hands. Momo rubbed her wrists to bring back the blood and to stop the pain of the rope. Now that the danger had passed she was shaking all over, but she kept up an appearance of calm.

"Come with me," said the boy, and led the way down the road and into a tea house that stood at the lower end of the bazaar—a real Tibetan tea house, Momo saw, where the mules of a caravan were bunching together in the mule yard outside the house. A large woman with kind black eyes and very red cheeks was standing over the stove.

"Here is a little girl from our land, O mother," said the boy. "She is very wet and shaken as a mouse that has just escaped from a trap. Give her some tea." The woman looked up and smiled at them, moved the pot she was stirring farther back on the stove, and came forward.

"You are indeed soaking wet, child," she said. "Come here by the fire." She pulled a low bench just before the great earthen stove, and both Momo and her own boy sat down with great content before the warmth and took the tea she poured for them. Momo sipped the hot, smooth tea, and felt its cheering warmth trickle down her throat and into her stomach, giving her strength and calm again. The kind woman moved from stove to table, serving the men there, talking cheerily with them, and yet keeping an eye on the two children before the fire too. Three times she filled their cups; then the boy spoke.

"Who are you, and how do you happen to let yourself be played upon by that rascal Tulsi?" he asked.

"I am Momo, from Longram. My father carries the post over

the top of the Jelep La, and I go to get back Pempa, my dog that was stolen from our house," she replied. "And how is it that you people from our sacred land are living here?"

"Oh," the boy answered, "we are here, in this steaming rain of the Sikkhim valleys, only during the wool season. My father is chief muleteer of a caravan, and my mother keeps a shop here, because it is a good place for business. This is, you know, the last bazaar where food can be bought, or corn for men and mules, until you come to the Chumbi valley towns. When the wool trains stop, we go back to our home in Khamba province."

Momo pulled off a tsampa bead, and began to suck it.

"Did you see my Pempa?" she asked eagerly. "A red-gold Lhasa terrier, carried along by five men, with a train of forty mules?"

The boy wrinkled his brow thoughtfully. "Yes," he said finally, "I did see them. I remember that dog and that train. They came by here yesterday morning in a furious hurry to be off and away again. They stole the dog, you say?" He laughed. "Well, your dog is giving the thief a very bad time," he went on. "Twice he has bitten the man's hand and so badly that it is bound—no one of them dares come near him. They throw food at him."

"Oh!" said Momo. "Good Pempa, I'm glad you fight! And I'm glad they feed him, too," she added. Just hearing of Pempa like that from a lad who had seen him only yesterday made him seem closer to Momo, and a wave of confidence went through her, warming her heart, and making her feel sure she would soon have her playmate back.

"Yes, they feed him well," the boy said. "They must. For when they arrive in Calcutta, if the dog is not in good condition, they will not be able to sell him."

"Sell!" cried Momo. "Where are they going to sell him—to whom?"

The boy looked at her with pity, but also with superiority, as if she were a little child.

"Go home, Momo," he said. "You cannot catch them now. They have a start over you of a day and a half, and they travel fast. They go by the train from Giellekhola tomorrow. And as soon as they reach Calcutta they take the dog and sell it."

Momo gasped. "Oh, where, to *whom*?" she cried, clasping her hands. "Tell me, tell me!"

The boy shook his head. "I don't know to whom," he replied. "Some great English lady there told your thief that if he could bring her a perfect Lhasa terrier, either black or gold, she would pay him one hundred rupees. And that is a very great deal of money," he added knowingly. "To get that for a dog! It is a fortune! No wonder they stole your Pempa!"

Momo jumped to her feet and stuffed her tea cup into her blouse. She felt on fire with energy and could hardly wait to be off again.

"I must hurry!" she said. "Thank you"—to the mother, and to the boy—"thank you for your great kindness to me. If it hadn't been for you they never could have caught that boy thief and set me free. When I come back I'll see you again. May you be rich, may all good come to you!" And before they could say a word, she shot away out into the rain and the gloom of the evening.

But she did stop to hear the boy shouting at her. "O Momo! Momo! Wait!" He was behind her, racing after her in the rain.

"If you must be such a little fool as to go on with this mad chase," he said, panting, "try to overtake my uncle. He just started off this afternoon, in a party of ten traders, all going down to Calcutta."

"Is he the man," Momo asked, "who knocked me down?"

The boy laughed. "Yes, that was my uncle," he said. "His name is Dorje; he is Big Dorje, and I am Little Dorje. I don't say that he is a very kind man, or that he will be glad to have you at his heels. But if you should happen into trouble on your way, you will at least—if you can catch up with them—have someone near you who can talk your own tongue."

"Oh, thank you! Great mercy," said Momo. "You are very kind. I'll try to catch them." And she turned and ran on out of the town and down the winding path toward the Rungi river and the swaying bridge which spanned it.

While she had been sitting in the tea shop the bazaar had ended. Even the last stragglers had left the town; the shouting and the tumult were over, and the only sounds were the rush of the rain and the roar of the Rungi river. The dark came on so quickly that Momo could hardly pick her way along the road. She heard rather than saw the river, when she approached it, and felt about with her hands for the guide ropes of the bridge.

Like all the bridges in this mountain world, this one had been easily made. Four bamboo poles were lashed together and slung from the steep hillsides across the stream, with a rope handrail to comfort the laden or the timid. So Momo felt about until she had both hands firmly on the guide ropes, then started across the river. The farther she went, the more the bamboo poles swayed; for every footstep seemed to set up a wave of motion that ran along to the farther bridge end. These waves followed so fast upon each other that they threw the whole length of the bamboo bridge into a tossing and swaying. Momo bounced up and down on the slippery poles as if she were

crossing a choppy sea. She hung tightly to the ropes, lest her foot slip off the round, wet bamboo poles, make her lose her balance, and plunge her headlong into the river below.

When she reached the opposite shore safely she drew a deep breath and decided to stop for the night. She had had enough. And a solitary light, shining with a golden radiance from a house not far away, was too tempting to pass by. Momo went toward it as surely as steel to a magnet. Inside she could see a woman standing by a stove. But with the memory of the dreadful house at Lingtam still fresh in her mind, she hardly dared enter, for fear the woman of the house would not let her stay. And how she dreaded a night out in this cold, wet world! She was so weary after all the travel and the excitement of the day that suddenly she felt she could not take another step. If they refused her admittance, she would lie down here, on their doorstep, like a dog, to sleep. So wistfully she stood out in the rain, looking in at the light, not daring to make herself known.

"O Holy Jewel in the Lotus!" she prayed, "make these people take me into their house tonight."

Then, as if in answer to this appeal, the woman of the house turned from the stove and looked out through the clouds of white smoke and saw Momo.

"Who are you, and what are you doing here?" she called.

Momo took one step inside the door.

"I am Momo, and I go down to the plains to get back my dog Pempa that was stolen from me."

The woman left her steaming kettle and came to the door. "Why, you are as wet as a drowned pig!" she said. "Come in, child, and dry by the fire." So Momo crept in thankfully and spread out her hands to the great stove's warmth.

"There! That is better. Come, give me your tea cup, little

Momo." And the kind woman filled Momo's cup with smoking hot tea. Momo sipped it slowly, to make it last longer. How good it tasted! She sighed in deep content and stretched out her feet to the fire. The cheering tea seemed to flow through her body in a warm and comforting way.

The woman of the house, who stood with folded hands watching her drink, looked down at her with pity. "Have you eaten, child?" she asked.

"I am hungry," Momo replied. And the kindly woman took a deep pot of vegetable stew from the stove, and a dish of curds, and put them on a little earthen ledge by the stove near the floor.

"Eat," she said, and with great satisfaction she watched Momo make a hearty dinner of the good hot food. Four times she filled the tea cup and four times Momo drained it. And then Momo stretched out like a dog on the floor by the stove. She felt now just pleasantly tired, and in the warmth did not mind her wet hair or clothes. The woman of the house smiled and said, "Now tell me again, child, just what you do on the Great Trade Route so late at night, and alone?"

So Momo told her story, and the woman sat on a bench beside her, and gave little cries of wonder and of sympathy as she listened. But she shook her head at the end, and said, "My child, for your mother's sake I wish you would turn back. Surely the trouble in the bazaar today shows you what dangers you may run into."

"You forget," Momo said, glad of the authority it gave her, "the prophecy. We are under the protection of the Blessed One, Pempa and I." But the woman only shook her head.

"If that is so," she replied, "go home, and leave it to Him to bring back your dog to you."

"No," said Momo obstinately. "I must go after Pempa. That is the prophecy." So the woman only looked at her sadly, and said no more.

"Who is this?" asked the man of the house, who had been sleeping behind the stove, and now, hearing their voices, sat up and looked about, rubbing his eyes.

"This is Momo, and she lives on the Jelep La pass. She goes now down to the plains to follow and find her dog that was stolen," replied the woman. The man frowned, and his wife said quickly, "See how much she is like our own little girl who died last year. Let her sleep here with us this night." And the man grunted and lay down again, but did not say no.

Momo had held her breath during this talk, for fear of being sent out into the wet dark. Now she smiled at the man, and spread out her hair to dry in the warmth. The motherly woman got a dry blanket, warmed it over the stove, and said, "Take off your wet robe, child, and roll yourself in this tonight. Then in the morning your own clothes will be dry." So with great thankfulness Momo slipped out of her heavy, wet woolen robe, and wrapped herself in the blanket. Then she lay down on the warm floor by the fire, and fell into a deep, restoring sleep.

Next morning, when the woman roused her, she found all her clothes, even her thick-soled boots, warm and dry.

"Come, get your tea and be off quickly," said the kindly woman. "Go as far as you can early today, for more rain will fall later this afternoon." Momo took her tea and bread and was soon ready.

"Thank you," she said. "Great mercy you have shown to me. I will not forget this kindness. May health be yours, and long life and wealth!" The woman nodded, and replied, "And may you come to the fulfillment of the prophecy, and no harm befall you!" And so, warm and dry and very cheerful from her breakfast of bread and tea, Momo started again on her chase.

Now in the bright fresh light of the dawn, she looked about in surprise to see the way she had come so stumblingly and haltingly in the dark of the night before. The little home that had sheltered her was only a stone's throw from the road, set in a little green paddy field on the flat valley floor. The Trade Route here was a fine stone causeway, crossing this valley from the bamboo bridge over the Rungi. But Momo turned her back on the river and the road of yesterday, to scan eagerly the path ahead. It led straight as an arrow up the steep hillside before her, and she walked it gladly.

Here the road's surface was more uneven; for the heavy rains had often rolled the stones away, leaving great holes; the earth too was washed away from what uneven boulders remained in place, and Momo had to climb and jump up from one stone to another. But neither she nor the mule trains that went clattering and chiming by minded the roughness of the way. They went up or down with a swing and a dash. Everything seemed to be full of joy just to be alive on such a beautiful sunny morning.

The road too was beautiful, and very open. It was fringed and shaded on both sides by a high and lovely forest of rhododendron trees and thickets of bright bamboo, clacking dryly in the breeze; and as she climbed higher Momo came into a noble grove of the white-flowering *pani-sal* tree, and the red-leafed *mowa*. There were graceful alders and beeches too, through whose gray trunks and green leaves she caught glimpses of the opposite hill, partly forested, partly terraced into little hill fields of rice or cardamom.

As Momo came to the top of the first ridge above the Rungi,

she jumped back in surprise. A band of Indian traders came
surging round the turn of the road, nearly knocking her over as
they plunged down the steep descent. Their feet were thrust,
bare-legged, into pointed, up-curling slippers, and their long
bony legs twinkled like scissors, cutting their way down the
mountainside. Each had a black umbrella hung from the neck
of his loose flying shirt, their white dhotis fluttered with the
speed of their downward passage, and they talked in a lively,
unceasing stream. In the second of their passing they looked
down on Momo with large dark eyes, friendly and incurious,
and were gone before she caught her breath.

Then for a while all travel stopped, and Momo walked alone.
The forest here was high and open. The leaves rustled lightly
in the breeze, and the sunlight, falling through their canopy,
made a moving pattern of light and shadow on the brown earth.
The air was sweet with the fragrance of the *pani-sal* blooms.
Momo was thinking what a happy, open, and friendly forest
this was, and how different from the one along the giant staircase. "That one," she said to herself, "was all silver mist. This
one is gold and light."

Suddenly she heard a shrill chattering above her head, and
looking up, saw a little gray creature swinging by a long tail
from the tree. It had a little black face, almost like a human being's, and soft gray fur round its neck like a ruff.

"A monkey!" thought Momo with a thrill. She had never
seen one before, but had often heard tales of the monkey people
of India. So she stood very still to watch. The little gray monkey
sat on the branch, her tail hanging free, and chattered again. As
if in reply, two little ones dropped down from an upper branch
and sat beside their mother.

Then, chattering all the while, the mother monkey wrapped

her tail round the tree limb, and hung down, headfirst; she let her body swing, first lightly and then more rapidly, and finally leaped to the next tree, catching hold of the bough with her tail, and swinging herself up to a sitting position. All these motions the mother went through, very slowly, three different times, while her babies sat on the bough and watched.

"Why, she's teaching the children to swing from one tree to another!" thought Momo, and she stared up at the monkey school in delight.

Now it was time for the children to practice the swing. Their mother sat close beside her babies, and putting her arm round the shoulder of the smaller one, seemed to be giving him the courage to begin. He dropped from the bough, hanging on by his tail, and leaped—but too soon—for the bough. He would have fallen to the earth if his mother had not quickly swung down and caught him, and lifted him back to safety. Then she sat beside him, chattering.

"She must be telling him what he did that was wrong," thought Momo. And she was full of joy when the mother gave the young one a little push, insisting that he make the try again, and at once.

Very unwillingly and timidly now, the little one dropped down and swung again. His mother screamed and screamed at him. "Harder, faster!" she was saying. And so obediently he swung back and forth till he got up a good speed, then took the leap—and landed on the limb in safety! Then such screams of praise and excitement as he got from the happy mother! Other monkeys higher in the trees that Momo had not seen before joined in the chorus of congratulations. And the little one sat proudly alone on his bough, laughing, sticking out and plucking at his furry neck, and making faces in his excitement.

Now only one baby monkey still sat there, not having tried the leap. He was the bigger one and the fatter of the two; but he was too lazy to learn. He only wanted to sit blinking in the sun. In vain his mother scolded and screamed at him. He would not budge. At last his mother lost her patience; she jumped beside him, and began biting and beating him, while his brother sat crying "Shame!" at him in a shrill baby voice. Still he sat there, cowering under the blows, but not moving. Momo laughed aloud.

"Why, you're as lazy as little Muni Tundoop, who won't help his father gather wood!" she cried. For the first time the monkeys noticed her. The mother screamed a warning, and before Momo had finished her words the family, even the fat and lazy one, had vanished, safely hidden and out of sight. Momo searched the forest for them, but in vain. She saw only the gray trunks and green leaves and heard only the leaves rustling lightly in the wind and the distant roar of the river.

"Oh, Pempa!" she cried, coming back to herself and her quest. "How shall I ever catch the thieves before they sell you if I keep on stopping like this?" And she fairly flew up the path. When she got to the top of that ridge of mountains, she could look down past a forested bit to an open hillside, and— Oh, joy! —there in the distance was her party of ten traders! One by one, Momo saw them emerge from the wood out into the open and slide down a steep incline to the grassy meadow. There each man took off his felt hat, and stripped to his waist, for this tropical jungle was very hot to these men of Tibet. Some ran to the stream near by and splashed themselves with water; some lay on the ground. Their cheery talk and laughter floated back through the clear, sweet mountain air to where Momo stood on the ridge.

"Now if they stop for a rest, I can overtake them here," she said to herself, and leaving the road, she took a straight line down the mountain, and went with a rush. She jumped from one rock to another, ducked under overhanging tree trunks, leaped across the stream when it crossed her path. And soon she too found herself catapulting out of the forest and into the open green meadow.

"Whew!" she said, sliding down the slippery bank to where all the men were lolling about.

"Hah!"

"Eh!"

"Oh!"

"What is this?" asked all the men, who were half asleep.

"I am Momo, and I live on the Jelep La, and I go down to Calcutta to get back my dog Pempa. They stole him from me, and mean to sell him in Calcutta," said Momo breathlessly.

She looked about till she saw and recognized the surly face of Little Dorje's uncle, and spoke to him.

"Little Dorje told me to hurry and catch up with you, so I wouldn't be alone when we get to the city," she finished.

The men looked at her in silence. Then Big Dorje spoke.

"Have you any money?"

"No," said Momo.

"Then you won't be able to get on the train at Giellekhola, and we won't be pestered long by you," he replied. And turning his back on her he stretched out again on the ground. Momo sat down at a little distance to wait.

"Just as Little Dorje said," she thought to herself. "Not polite. But I don't care, if only they don't stop here long. I want to go on and catch those thieves." So she sat waiting impatiently, till finally the traders jumped up, put on their robes, slapped their felt caps upon their heads, and started off. Momo jumped up too, and followed after them like a little dog.

The ten traders walked like the wind, without effort, up one mountainside, and down the other, up the next mountain-side, and down that. And each new mountain ridge was a little less high, for they were leaving behind them the great mountain peaks, white with eternal snow, and coming down and down, by crossing lesser mountain ranges, toward the great plains of India. Between these mountain ranges lay little valleys, cut out by swift-flowing green rivers; and each valley they crossed was nearer to sea level, hotter, with the steamy, sticky heat of the tropics.

This was quite new to Momo. In all her life she had never been so hot. Sometimes, when she had stood by their hot stove, baking cakes for her mother, she had felt herself burning up; but if she ran to the door she was cooled in a few moments by the keen air. Here, in these pretty valleys which twisted through the hills like green serpents, she learned what it is to be really hot. Sweat poured from her in an unending river; it ran down into her eyes, it stuck her hair to her forehead, it made her heavy woolen dress more heavy and scratchy.

"Ooof! I am hot!" she said, wiping her face. But the men did not stop nor speak, and she ran on again after them, like a little dog. In the late afternoon clouds rolled up suddenly from the south, black and menacing, and soon rain fell, in a heavy, soaking, steady downpour. And still it was hot—not quite so hot as when the sun shone, but still hot and more muggy than before. Momo felt stifled; she could hardly breathe. Her feet slipped on the wet clay road, and twice she fell, and went coasting down the hillside through the mud and the wet. But the traders paid her no heed, only went plodding on themselves, chatting and laughing. And so Momo picked herself up, wiped the mud off her hands on her robe, and the rain and the hair out of her eyes, and followed grimly behind them.

Toward nightfall the traders stood on the top of a mountain ridge leading down to Rhenok. There, from what they said to each other, Momo understood they would stop the night. And so, eager to rest and get out of the rain, the ten men went down this last hillside in a whirlwind, with Momo close behind. It was nearly dark when they came into the pretty little town of Rhenok, which stretched its little wooden houses along the two forks of a road, and had its center and heart where the two roads came together. In spite of the rain the town was a lively spot. Men and women were passing from one house to another, small boys and girls played and shouted at each other in the rain, or took shelter now and again under the overhanging eaves of a house. Here, also sheltering from the rain, were flocks of hens, and a goat or two.

All the people here seemed cheerful. They called and laughed to each other in passing, and the little lamps lighted in their homes shone like bright yellow gold in the gloom of the darkening street. Momo looked hopefully at each house as they walked through the town, but the traders strode on and on, till at the very outskirts of the village they came to one last house. It was, she saw with a sinking heart, the oldest and dirtiest of them all. But the men stamped up the steps, crossed the verandah, and one of them stuck his head in the open door, shouting, "Ho! Sister Dolma! Here is your brother, and a party of friends going down to the plains to trade."

"Come in, brother. Come in, all," a woman replied in a harsh and rasping voice. Momo trembled at the sound.

"A good heart and a sweet voice go together," she thought.

"What can I expect in kindness from this ugly voice?" But she followed the men inside and stood timidly near the door. The men took off their heavy caps, loosened their heavy robes, and sat down to the table. They all pulled out their tea cups, waiting eagerly for the hot drink.

"This is not a tea shop, you know," said the woman in a whining voice, "so you must be content with what we have. Here is only bread and curds," and she set two dishes on the table, and filled their tea cups. No one of the men offered Momo a place at the table, or paid any attention to her. But she was so hungry and chilled that at the sight of the food and the tea she crept forward, with her cup in her hand. The woman of the house looked at her in surprise.

"Now which one of you," she asked the men, "is the foolish father who will drag a child like this on a trading journey to the plains?" Big Dorje looked up.

"Nothing to do with us," he replied roughly. "The little fool thinks that she can get to Calcutta to find her dog, which was stolen from her home."

The woman set down her copper teapot and stared at Momo. "What's that, child?" she asked. "Who are you, and what do your parents think of this fine journey of yours?" So Momo had to tell her story again before all the traders. She started boldly, but even her faith in the prophecy and the protection of the Blessed One could not keep her voice strong in the face of their contempt and disbelief. Dolma too stared at her as if she thought Momo a very naughty child. But when Momo stopped, almost trembling, she was amazed to hear the woman say only, "Come then, sit down, and drink." And she poured her a cup of tea.

Momo ate a piece of the bread and scooped out a handful of

curds when all the traders had finished. Then she slipped over near the fire and sat on the floor. The man of the house and Dolma were talking with Big Dorje, but Momo was so tired that she sat in a ball, with her head on her knees and her arms clasping her legs, and thought only of sleep. But her head jerked up when she heard her father's name mentioned.

"Nema, the dak runner of the Jelep La, of course I know," said Dolma, in her rasping voice. "Did he not work in Kalimpong for the Lat Sahib before he got this job of the post?" Her husband nodded.

"Well, then," she went on, "we will send the child back home. It is even more danger than folly for such a one to be walking alone down into the city of Calcutta."

"Ugh!" said Big Dorje. "No fear. She will never get beyond Kalimpong, or the train station at Giellekhola." The woman tossed her head, and sniffed.

"And what makes you think, O Dorje," she asked scornfully, "that no harm could befall the child in the big bazaar town of Kalimpong, or the station at Giellekhola? No. it is settled. The trader travels into the hills with a load of brick tea for Lhasa; he starts tomorrow, and the child shall go with him."

On hearing these words, Momo's heart dropped like a stone, and for a moment she felt too weak to move. Then she was afire with a passionate need for escape; but even in her great fear she was prudent enough not to draw attention to herself. For some time longer she sat very still, listening to the plans Dolma made for sending her back; then, when she could stand it no longer. she began slowly edging away from the fire, out of the group lying and sitting about there, nearer and nearer the door. No one noticed her, and with a sigh of great thankfulness she rose, and set one foot over the threshold. A second more, and she would be free.

But the watchdog barked. He jumped to his feet, blocking her passage, growling at her furiously. Momo tried in vain to slip past him.

"What's that?" cried Dolma, and in a second Big Dorje reached out and dragged her, screaming and kicking, back into the room, before the fire.

"O ungrateful one!" exclaimed Dolma angrily. "You drink the tea and eat the food of this house, and then without thanks, you slip off like a thief in the night! May I take your ill luck if I do not send you back home! Tomorrow morning early you start off with a strong man who will carry you back to your parents. And now sleep here." And to make sure that Momo did not try again to escape in the night, she took a piece of rope and tied one end to Momo's waist, the other round her own ankle. Then the whole household settled themselves for the night, the traders rolled up in their blankets on the floor, the man and the woman of the house near the big stove, with Momo between them—tied fast.

V. THE TEN TRADERS AND TSU FOO

The house was very still; there was only the steady patter of rain on the roof, and the deep, regular breathing of the people on the floor. Momo alone, in a turmoil of anger and fear, breathed in short, choking gasps. Her head was spinning with thoughts of escape. Once she tried very gently to untie the knot of the rope round her waist; but even the least pull on the rope gave a tug at the end tied round Dolma's ankle and, half waking, she growled at her to lie still.

Even if she should get free of the rope, how could she pass the dog, who through the dark hours of night was at his most watchful? No one could enter the house without his raising a clamor, no one but his master or mistress could go out without an equal uproar. Momo lay still and listened to the rain; and presently she drew comfort from its steady drumming. After all, for the moment she was snugly warm, and so sleepy from the long day in the open that her breathing too became more even and her body relaxed.

"O blessed Jewel in the Lotus," she prayed, "O Mother Tara, if indeed it is your will that I get Pempa back, lend me your help and free me from this woman—in your own time and your own way." And then she rolled over and slept like a log until in the half-light of the dawn the household came to life. The ten traders jumped to their feet, stretching and yawning, and pulled up their robes, tying them tighter around their waist. They lit cigarettes and sat smoking and chatting, watching Dolma work, and waiting for their tea.

She was the first one up, pulling Momo with her. "Come, get up, sleepy one!" she called, giving a twitch to the rope. And perforce Momo followed her about, like a dancing bear on the chain of a wandering player. She helped carry in wood to feed the fire, ladled water into the pots for boiling, and shortly the tea was hot and ready to drink. Immediately afterward, the traders slapped their caps upon their heads, made their farewells, and were off, striding down the hillside. Dolma stood in the doorway, with Momo very doleful and uneasy at her side, to see them off, and then she went about her morning's work. With every passing moment, Momo became more impatient, but she forced herself to appear calm, and to await the right moment for escape.

"It must come, it *must!*" she kept repeating to herself.

But the moments and the hours slipped by, and Dolma made no attempt even to take Momo out to the trader who was going up to Lhasa. Instead, she set the child to picking over dried beans, and washing rice. Then she made her pile wood and watch the fire. The sun was high, the morning already half gone. Finally Momo could endure it no longer.

"Where is the trader for Lhasa?" she asked. "Aren't you going to take me to him?"

Dolma gave an unpleasant laugh. "There are many caravans going up the Great Trade Route in this wool season," she said. "You are a strong child, and work well. I, who have no children to help me, can use you very nicely for a time. Why should I cast off such help, when the country gods and the hills provide it? Come now," she went on, tugging sharply at the rope, so that she jerked Momo to her feet, "get to work! You will not earn your tea by sitting there like a lady. Lift this pot of water to the stove, to heat."

At these words, Momo's hot temper flared up. Anger swept through her like a burning fire. And quick as fire, without stopping to plan or to think, she lifted the heavy copper pot and flung the water full in Dolma's face. Then, seizing the big household knife from the table, she cut the rope that tied her fast, and dashed out of the door and down the steps. She was running down the road before Dolma could catch her breath.

Behind her as she fled, Momo heard her sputtering and choking from the cold water, then running after her, screaming at her to stop, and calling upon the villagers to help her in the chase. But Dolma was fat and unused to running, while Momo was as fleet as the wind. She looked back once and laughed to see Dolma's fat and shapeless figure struggling down the road, then, still boiling over with anger, she leaped down the mountainside.

"Half the morning lost, and the traders—how far ahead of me?" she fumed. "Shall I be able to overtake even them again?

And Pempa—it is *today* that he is, Little Dorje said, going down to the plains! Oh, let me speed!"

Never had she covered the ground so rapidly. Luckily the road here was broad and in fine repair, the cobbles all in place, and the grades, though steep, not so nearly vertical as those along the giant staircase. The rain had stopped in the early morning, and all the earth was fresh and green, raindrops still glinting in the sun. In this bright and golden light it was impossible to be angry long. Momo lifted her face to the blue sky, felt the warm breeze brush softly against her cheek, and was again full of joyous confidence.

"By the Lord's will," she murmured, "I will get Pempa back." And with a mind at peace, she began again to observe the world through which she journeyed. "Every day different," she said to herself.

She was dropping down to the stream bed of the Resi river through a forest wonderful with tree ferns and bamboo groves and rushing waterfalls. At every step she caught different and entrancing glimpses of the Resi and its high, winding walls. Here the great forests had been cleared. Sturdy farmers had cut the hillsides into terraces that rose step by step from the valley, and followed the curving line of the hill. All these terraces were bright with the green of rice and millet. And stuck like burrs into the hillside were the comfortable farmhouses, with pink walls and overhanging thatched roofs. Momo had never seen anything so beautiful.

While she stopped to gaze at this rich green farm land, rising in tiers to the sky—so different from her own Tibetan farms!—there was a rustle at her side, and up through the bamboo and onto the road came a quick gliding file. They were the people of the hills on their way to market. Young men and old men, old women and young women, boys and girls, and babies hanging at their mothers' hips—everybody who lived on the hill was moving down to the bazaar, and carrying some goods to market. Momo had never seen *people* carry things like this before. Now and then, it is true, the poorest Tibetan peddlers would go up and down the trade road with packs on their backs; but mostly people tucked what they wanted to carry into saddle packs, and hung them on each side of a yak or a mule.

"Why," she thought to herself in surprise, "they are making *mules* of themselves!"

She looked curiously at one family that was just coming up on the road. An old grandfather walked first and set the pace. Then came the father, a little boy four or five years old, and two very pretty girls. Every one of them walked bending forward from the weight of the basket he carried on his back. Momo stared at the boy, who followed his father, taking each little step, toeing in, exactly like his father. His basket, she saw, was just like all the others—as long as his back, and narrow at the bottom, then widening until at the shoulders it was as broad as he was. And like all the others, the boy carried the basket by a wide strap round his forehead. Only the father carried heavy potatoes, and the little boy light spinach leaves.

As they came up to the main road, where Momo stood staring, the girls set their heavy baskets on a stone ledge, and took away the strap from their foreheads, to rest. But the men set walking sticks under the bottom of their loads, and bent almost double, so that the stick supported their baskets.

"Ugh!" said the grandfather.

"Ugh!" said the father, mopping his brow.

"Ugh!" repeated the little boy, in his high childish voice. The women said nothing at all.

Momo stared at the girls, the prettiest she had ever seen, with golden skin and a red hibiscus blossom stuck into the knot of their smooth black hair. She admired their wide figured skirts of red and yellow, that swung like bells when they walked, and their heavy silver necklaces and bracelets and the tinkling anklets that they wore about their little feet. "How rich they must be!" she thought. And then, as they took up their loads again, she ran on ahead of them down toward the river.

The nearer she came to it, the steeper was the way, the louder and sweeter the rush of the waterfalls, the deeper the roar of the river; and beating insistently through these sounds was the ceaseless music of the cicadas, who live in the moist river valleys. When first she heard the air vibrating with their chirps, Momo stopped and looked about. Then she remembered that the muleteers spoke of this constant whirring song in the tropical river valleys; it was made, they said, by a kind of tree cricket, never seen, but always heard.

"Ah!" she cried aloud, like one greeting a friend, "Cicadas!" And she took joy in their steady hum, which went with her down to the clear Resi river, across an iron bridge—a wonder that, to Momo, who had never seen one like it!—up a bit of forest on the opposite hill, and only died away when she came out into open farm land.

Now she was moving up through those terraces she had admired from afar, and she saw that the rice was heading. In this world of heavy rainfall water was everywhere. It stood in all the little terraces, so that the green rice spears rose from silver lakes. The water spilled over from one terrace to fall into the next, so that the whole hill, when she saw it closely, was a gentle waterfall.

"How wonderful, this water! And running to waste, too!" Momo said to herself. "No marvel that they have such fruits and vegetables. Ah, how I wish I could send this stream of water up to Uncle Muni!" She felt sad to think how hard he and all the farmers of Tibet worked over their tiny ditches, to save and direct the slenderest trickle of precious water over their scanty crops. Even her own home in the slope of the Jelep La, which had sufficient rainfall, and was not, like the great plain of Tibet, dry as a bone—even her home was not like this world of silver rain and rivers and dense greenery.

"Things grow so fast!" she thought, feeling the quick pulse of life in these tropical hills and valleys. And while she marveled at the jungle growth, she found herself running out upon the street of the thriving bazaar town of Pedong.

"Here I might find the traders," she said to herself, "if, that is, they have been lazy and chose to sit talking in a tea shop." She scanned each house, and all the people in the street, but her party was not there. So on she hurried.

Beyond Pedong the road was wider, smoother, and much more level. Instead of rising in short zigzags up one side of a steep mountain, and falling straight as a plumb line down the other, the Great Trade Route here moved in gentle sweeping lines about much lower hills. On this easy grade Momo traveled, though without seeming to hurry, at great speed. In a short time she had reached the ancient trading post of Aligarrah.

At the entrance to the town, her road joined another, and in this triangular forking of the roads was the market place, now a scene of busy trading. Momo looked longingly at the piles of yellow bananas and green squash, but did not linger. To-day she had not even time to spend in gazing. Between the brown, two-storied houses that twisted with the trade route round the hill, she went. Cautiously she peeped into the tea shops to look for the traders, but after her experience with Dolma, she did not dare to enter.

"Oh," she said to herself, "for a cup of hot tea!" But she pulled off a tsampa bead to suck, and when she had got out of the town, drank from a running stream. So on and on, up and round the terraced hills and the thatched pink houses she went, while the sun dropped lower in the sky, and threw its light more slantingly and more golden upon the green rice. The day was over when she came out upon a ridge and looked across a wide valley up to a massive snow range.

One central peak towered into the middle heaven, and all the snows were pink in the light of the setting sun. It was so wonderful, and such a surprise, that Momo gasped. Then she bent her head in reverence. For this mightiest snow mass, she knew, was Kinchenjunga, a goddess of great power, and widely worshiped. The goddess's head and those of her sister peaks were gleaming in the sunlight, but shadows were already creeping up from the valleys, casting every moment higher and deeper purple veils over the lower ranges. Soon it would be dark, and before then she must be in Kalimpong.

And there, surely, it lay below her—filling the seat of the saddle she had come out upon! For she stood at one tip of a long mountain ridge, which dipped gently down, and then rose again at the other end. And midway between these two high points, in the gentle seat of this broad saddle, was a great massing of houses. They stretched far along the ridge, and spilled down the mountainside. Momo's eyes sparkled, and her breath came in quick, excited puffs.

Kalimpong. Where all the wool caravans reached their

journey's end! Where in the great bazaar the muleteers wandered from shop to shop, buying here turquoise-studded charm boxes for their wives to wear round their necks, there coral nose drops for their daughters, and for themselves fine blankets striped in gay colors! Everything in the world that a man might want, her father and the muleteers agreed, you would find in the bazaar at Kalimpong.

As she paused to look down upon the town, the pink sunset glow faded from the great snow mountains, and the purple shadows rose higher. So, full of joyous anticipation, Momo danced along the ridge, and came into the town. She hardly knew where to begin to look, everything was so wonderful. Most of all she was caught by the air of brisk and lively business. Greater buildings she had seen, at Sera and the other monasteries of her land, and in the city of Gyantse and the capitol at Lhasa; but never before had she found trade to be anything but the exchange of local goods. Here she felt the rapid pulse of big important business.

Momo stood quite still and let this busy life of the bazaar flow through her. She loved it; her black eyes picked up each least detail, and her keen mind stored them up to remember. Like all her people, Momo was born with a keen sense for trade. She and her mother made a game of counting the wool caravans' loads, and reckoning their total weight of wool. From day to day they carried over, in their heads, a tally of what wool had gone past their home, and down to Kalimpong. At the end of the season, when the muleteers came back, they talked of the price that had been paid for wool; of what the herdsmen had got for their fleece; they guessed accurately at the profit taken by the wool middlemen or merchants in Rinchengong, and of what the costs of the caravan transport had been. And so, little as she was, Momo knew as well as a man the value of her country's trade in wool.

"And here," she said to herself, in the great satisfaction of one who sees things actually happen, "*here,* in this very bazaar, they make this trade. Here the wool comes in, and turns into money; and that money turns into salt and brick tea, rice and oil, to go back over the passes into Tibet. And all the muleteers spend their wages here."

Not only muleteers but all the world seemed to be thronging the bazaar. The Tibetans she expected to see; but here were also men from Ladak, beyond the northern Himalayas; from Marwar, the Punjab, Bengal, and Kabul—all different in looks and dress, all here to trade their goods for the money brought by Tibetan wool. Since it was Saturday, the people of the countryside were here too in great numbers, all the women in brilliant shawls and saris. The open shops flooded the street with yellow light from their lamps or torches, and the people walked through it like a moving rainbow.

"How dull our clothes are!" thought Momo for the second time on her journey, and she looked with disfavor on her dark grayish robe. "These hill women are as bright as parakeets." She stared in wonder at their great earrings, which covered their ears, and hung in pendants to their shoulders. With chains, amulets, rings, nose drops, and anklets, every woman was loaded with jewelry, mostly of silver, studded with turquoise or coral.

The shops too Momo studied, passing slowly from one end of the bazaar to the other. She was fascinated by the Indian bankers, sitting on their clean white-sheeted floors, and leaning against great cushions. Their money, kept in safes, was in an inner room, protected from street thievery by iron grills. The

goldsmiths too sat behind bars, puffing at their blow-pipes, or fashioning the precious metal into a flower-like nose drop for some hill beauty. There were shops filled with shining brass and copper pots, water jars, and bowls for cooking and eating; others packed with the bright sari cloth or fine embroidered wool shawls; there were toys—wonderful dolls and bears and balls; soaps, sweet scents, umbrellas, shoes, and lanterns. And most of these things Momo had never in her life seen before. She almost forgot her search for Pempa and the ten traders in her wonder and excitement.

It was the smell of food from the food shops at the end of the bazaar that made her remember the men for whom she was searching.

"Ah!" she chided herself. "Suppose now the traders have gone early to sleep. How shall I find them?" And she began running up and down, looking at every Tibetan she passed. At last, following a muleteer to see if he might not lead her to a Tibetan inn, she found her party. They were sitting in the open, at a little distance from the bazaar, and playing a gambling game by the light of a flickering torch. Momo crouched down out of sight, watching and waiting. She felt very sleepy, but forced her eyes to stay open, removed a tsampa bead and sucked it, while she kept herself awake by saying her prayers upon the string of cheese beads as on a rosary.

When at last their game ended, and the men rose and strode down through the town, Momo was at their heels, unobserved. She watched them enter an inn, and then settled herself in the doorway.

"This time," she told herself, "I'll not give myself up to any greedy innkeeper." And so she curled herself into a ball like a hedgehog, prepared to sleep in the open. "If I stay here in the door," she thought, "they can't leave without stumbling over me—and I cannot miss them!" Weary as she was, Momo was fast asleep in a moment. But after a time the door opened behind her, and a girl, coming out, stumbled and fell over Momo.

"Oh!" she cried softly. "What is this?"

"Oh! Did I hurt you? I am sorry," said Momo, helping her to her feet.

"No, I am not hurt," replied the girl, in her soft voice. "But who are you, and what do you do here?"

"I am Momo, and I follow the ten traders, who sleep in your house, down to Calcutta. I go there to find my dog Pempa, that was stolen from me," said Momo, still sleepy.

"But why do you stay here in the doorway?" asked the girl again.

"Because I have no money for a night's lodging, and I must stay here, or I may lose them in the morning, of course," replied Momo.

"Come," said the girl. "You may sleep with me if you like. Here it is cold, and the mists will be thick and wet."

"But suppose I miss the traders?" asked Momo, stretching herself, and thinking how very pleasant it would be to get out of this chill night air, and lie flat to sleep.

The girl laughed sadly. "You cannot miss them if they sleep in this house," she said. "For I am Tsu Foo, and I do all the hard work of this house. They wake me while it is still black night, and make me get up to bring in water for tea, and wood to start a fire."

"Then I'll come gladly with you, and thank you," Momo answered. So she followed the girl up a flight of outside stairs that led to a little garret room under the roof. It had one tiny window, one straw pallet, and nothing more. Both girls lay

down on the narrow bed, and drew up a rough cover over them.

"How thin you are!" cried Momo. "You're just bones, aren't you?"

"Yes," said the girl sadly. "I'm always hungry; they starve me here."

"I have plenty of food," said Momo. "Here, take some of my cheese to suck."

"How good!" said Tsu Foo hungrily. "Thank you."

Momo lay for a moment wondering about Tsu Foo. She talked in a sing-song like the Chinese traders who sometimes came up over the passes into Tibet, carrying dried fish from China and rich brocaded silks for wealthy Tibetans to have made into robes.

"You aren't Tibetan, are you?" she asked.

"No," replied Tsu Foo. "I am the child of a Chinese father and a Nepali mother. My father and mother were very good to me, but last year they both died of a sickness that came over this town."

"Oh, I am sorry," said Momo, thinking suddenly of her own dear mother, and her jolly, kind father, and of how much she loved them, and how dreadful it would be to have them both suddenly gone.

"My father owned this fine tea shop and hostel for the Tibetans who come through Kalimpong," Tsu Foo went on, talking with her mouth full of the cheese bead. "He left it to my mother's brother, Lop San, and told him to take care of the place for me, and give it to me when I am old enough to marry. But Lop San is very cruel, and his wife too; they both want this place for themselves alone, and so they treat me as badly as they possibly can. They hope to make me so tired of being beaten and made to do all the hard work that one day I will run away. Then they will have the tea house to themselves."

"That is very evil of them," said Momo indignantly. "How can they expect to win merit and gain a better birth in their next life if they do such evil in this one?"

"They do not think of any other life but this," replied Tsu Foo. "And to tell you the truth, neither do I. I work so hard I have no time to think, and at night I am too tired even to pray." She drew a deep sigh. "But perhaps I will run away, some day," she added half to herself.

"Come down with me to Calcutta," said Momo quickly. "Everyone in all the world goes there to work, and finds it, so the muleteers say."

But Tsu Foo shook her head. "Not now," she said. "I am afraid, for I have no money, and no clothes but these rags I have on. Besides, I have just had fever and am too weak for such a journey. But what matter if I die along the way? If I stay here much longer, I must die anyhow of work and starvation." Her voice dropped away, as if she were too weak even to speak more.

Momo bounced up and down in the rough straw bed with rage and pity. "Oh!" she cried, "How I wish I might set my Pempa on your uncle—he would soon frighten him into some decency! But you are right—stay here now, and I will find a place for you down there in that great city. Then you can go safely, knowing that friends and work will await you."

"Do you know any people there?" asked Tsu Foo, "that you can speak so surely?"

"No," replied Momo. "But the Blessed One has us in His care, and He will lead me to those who will give you help. Have no fear of that."

"I will wait," said Tsu Foo, "and I thank you for giving me

some hope. But now let us sleep, or they will wake me before I have taken any rest." And weary as both were, in a moment they were fast asleep with their arms round each other.

As Tsu Foo had said, she was wakened, and in no gentle manner. It seemed to Momo that she had hardly closed her eyes when a man's rough voice called up the steps: "Come, get up, lazy child of a worthless father! If I have to come after you, I'll kick you downstairs."

"Coming!" called Tsu Foo. And to Momo she whispered, "Stay here till I have gone, then go down to the street. He must not know you have been here."

Momo nodded, and flinging her arms round Tsu Foo's thin little body, she whispered, "Have no fear. I'll come back with a place for you." Then Tsu Foo fled. And lying on the rough bed, Momo flamed into furious anger when she heard Lop San box his niece's ear, and say by way of greeting, "One second longer, and you'd have come down these stairs head first! Get out to the well and bring in water for tea!"

She ground her teeth, and thought in amazement, "How is it possible that Tsu Foo has endured such ill treatment for so long? I would *kill* him!" She jumped silently to her feet, waited till all was quiet below, and then, peering carefully about, to make sure that she was not observed, she ran lightly down the steps and stood in the street. Not daring to stand too close, she loitered up and down the opposite side of the street, and finally sat down on the edge of the road, to await her traders.

She hoped too for a glimpse of the cruel Lop San, and of Tsu Foo. Nor was she disappointed. When the ten traders came out of the inn, Lop San came too, and stood in the doorway watching them start. He was a short but very strongly built man, with a heavy, brutish face, and as Momo looked at him, she repeated to herself a Buddhist proverb often on her mother's lips: " 'Whatever is unpleasant to yourself, do not do to another.' " And looking with indignant anger at his coarse face, she muttered, "Take care, Lop San! *In this life* you shall pay for your evil deeds!"

Then, as she started after the traders, she noticed Tsu Foo's thin, pale little face peeping out at her from the back door of the house. She smiled at her and ran down the street after the men, even more eager to reach Calcutta than before, since she now had two missions to perform. The ten traders went stamping along the fine wide street of the town, unconscious of their little shadow, and came out upon a curving road, with a shiny black surface at which Momo wondered greatly. This road had been built by the Indian government for motor cars to travel on, and they passed several on their way.

When Momo saw the first of these—a great black monster that came rushing up at her, faster than the fastest yak can run —she was too frightened to move, but stood still in its path, frozen with terror. A man sitting within, she saw, and he blew a loud and angry blast on a horn. At that Momo leaped for safety to the trees by the roadside; and none too soon, she thought to herself, as the great black beast or demon whizzed past her, raising a cloud of dust. She sank to the ground in a heap, and panted with fright. The traders, she saw with amazement, walked quietly along the side of the road, as if this whizzing monster had been only a yak-drawn cart. So she tried to act like them; but when next one of these monsters came rushing at her, Momo jumped quickly into the forest by the roadside—and then felt foolish, as she saw all the other people plodding steadily along, paying it no attention whatever.

The muleteers had talked, she recalled, of these motor cars

that went like the wind, without yak or mule to draw them; but although the idea had delighted her, Momo had always secretly believed that they could not really be true. Now with her own eyes she had seen, and her head was spinning with the marvel of it. After a time she lost her fear, but was very careful still to give these motor cars the whole of the road, when they came rolling along.

Many people besides the traders and herself were walking the road. Men and women came from all the little farms on the hillside, carrying their vegetables and fruits up to the bazaar at Kalimpong. Another line of people moved with Momo down the road, carrying bundles, baskets, and boxes to be put upon the train at Giellekhola. They all had something to take down to the plains, and they all must have, as Momo suddenly realized, money to buy themselves a seat on this train.

"How shall I be taken on this *te-rain,* without money for a *tikkut?*" Momo asked herself, and the shadow of a doubt ruffled the smooth trust of her mind. But she quickly smoothed it out again, with the thought, "He who has given me Pempa, and who has protected me so far, will find a way."

At last she saw beneath her a strange road, with two straight lines like shining snakes stretched taut along it. There was a house; and in front of this house, standing on these two shining bars, in the middle of the strange road she saw the train. *"Te-rain!"* she murmured to herself in joy. She knew it at once, for as the kind woman of the tea shop had said, it was a great black creature, breathing a cloud of dense black smoke, like a dragon. And behind it here was a line of little houses strung together like beads. These, Momo surmised, must be where the people sat when the big black dragon pulled them down the hills.

Indeed, some people were already sitting in these carriages, she saw, as she followed the traders up to the platform. There were crowds of people standing about, sitting on their boxes, drinking tea, talking; and at the end of the train, next to the black dragon, men were busily loading boxes and crates into one of the carriages. Momo dodged through the crowds and, sticking closely behind the traders, followed them up to a window in the front of the big house. Each man laid down some money, and came away with a little red ticket. When Big Dorje stepped away from the booth, with his ticket, Momo spoke to him, timidly.

"Oh, Big Dorje, give me the money for a *tikkut*, and I will pay you back." He looked down at her and growled, "May I die before sunset! Here is that brat again."

Momo clasped her hands beseechingly. "Oh, give me the money—*lend* me only enough for a *tikkut*," she cried. "My father will pay you for it when I get home." Big Dorje laughed contemptuously.

"Oh, then *I* will pay you," Momo pleaded. "I will go and work for you, I can herd sheep and yaks, and do all the work of a house."

But Big Dorje pushed her away without a word and moved toward the train after the other traders. They had already taken their places in the tiny carriages and were sprawling on the wooden seats. The train began to puff and snort, it threw up a rumbling black cloud of smoke, a shrill whistle blew, and the station master gave a warning call. All on the station platform jumped to confusion and hurry. The people who were going on the train and had not yet got aboard rushed for the nearest carriage, and squeezed themselves in; the sweetmeat-sellers and the tea-venders shouted their wares louder than before, in their last moment's chance of selling.

Big Dorje swung himself into one of the little carriages and sat down, still paying no more heed to Momo than if she had not been there, looking pleadingly at him from the platform. Again the train gave a shrill warning whistle. In this last moment of departure the noise and confusion became still greater. Big Dorje slammed the door of his carriage in Momo's face. And at that last unkindness, when she saw the train actually ready to go off without her, Momo threw back her head, screwed up her eyes, and cried—not in easy tears, but great strangling sobs that seemed to tear the very heart out of her breast.

VI. PROTECTOR OF THE POOR

"What is the matter?"

Momo opened her eyes upon a tall British gentleman standing before her. He was studying her with keen blue eyes. And, what even at that moment filled her with astonishment, he was speaking to her in her own Tibetan tongue. Momo gulped back a rising sob, and stuck out her tongue at him. Even in her misery and astonishment, she remembered her manners enough to make him this, the most respectful greeting a poor Tibetan can give to one of high rank.

"Do you want to get on this train?" asked the gentleman. Momo nodded, still shaken by her sobbing, and gasped out one word, "Calcutta!" Then the tall gentleman looked off to where the station master was watching him and raised his right hand. The station master nodded and ran up toward the engine to talk to the engineer, who could see everything from where he stood in his open cab.

"Now," the gentleman went on, turning again to Momo. "Tell me, child. Why are you traveling to Calcutta? And where are your father and mother?"

By this time Momo had control over her voice, and she replied, "I am Momo, and I live near the top of the Jelep La pass. My father carries the mails, and my mother keeps a tea shop in Longram. And I go down to Calcutta to get back my dog Pempa, who was stolen from our house."

"You have come all this way alone?" asked the man.

"Yes, I have come alone," Momo answered. "The last two days I have followed those ten traders, because Little Dorje told me they go to Calcutta. They know that great city, and they speak my tongue, so I thought they might help me find Pempa when we get down to Calcutta. But"—and her face puckered up again, and tears flowed down her cheeks—"I have no money, and cannot buy a *tikkut* to get on the *te-rain*."

The tall gentleman looked at her in silence. Finally he said, "My child, you have courage. Do you love this Pempa of yours enough to brave the dangers of that great, strange city of Calcutta? Enough not to fear getting lost or stolen?"

"Oh, yes, yes," Momo replied. "I am not at all afraid. The Holy One will keep me from all harm. I know that. And I thought He was going to put me on this *te-rain* today. But," she gulped back another sob, "He has not done so."

The blue eyes that looked searchingly into her black ones were very bright as the gentleman said, "Ah, but your faith is rewarded, little Momo. The Blessed One is even now going to put you on this train, acting through me, His unworthy agent."

He took her by the hand and walked with her up to the ticket window, where he laid down some money, and took up the red ticket the agent handed him. This he put into Momo's hand.

"There is the ticket," he said. "Hold to it tightly, Momo, and do not let it out of your hands till you pass out of the gate on the station platform at Siliguri. There you must follow the other travelers and buy still another ticket for Calcutta. Just stand before the window, lay down this money"—he put some silver in her hand—"and say these words, 'One ticket to Calcutta.' Can you do that, do you think?"

Momo's hand closed tightly over the money, and she nodded her head. "Yes, yes, I can. One *tikkut* to Calcutta. That is easy," she said. Her face was shining like the sun after a rain.

"Good," said the strange gentleman. "Now listen carefully, Momo. When you come to the city of Calcutta, you will need more money. Take this," and he handed her more silver and one paper note. "Tie this into your scarf, and *tell no one that you have any money.* Do you understand? Do not open your scarf and show your money where you may be watched by strangers. For in Calcutta there are many quick and clever thieves." Again he repeated, "Do you understand?"

"Yes, yes," Momo nodded. "I do understand, and I will remember your warning, great sir." Her fingers worked quickly as she tied the money into a corner of her red scarf, and tucked the scarf into the fold of her robe.

"Very well," said the gentleman. "You now have money enough, Momo, to take you down to the city, and give you food and lodging there in some Tibetan hostel, and help you make inquiries about your dog. There is also money for your return ticket back to the hills. So if you are wise and careful, you should have no further trouble—only the finding of your dog."

"And the Blessed One Himself will do that, when I get to the city," answered Momo happily.

"We must in any case leave that to Him," replied the tall gentleman with a smile. He led her along the platform, looking into the carriages as they passed.

"Where are those ten traders you spoke of?" he asked her, and Momo looked and said, "There they are, in this, and this carriage. And here," she added, "here is Big Dorje, whom Little Dorje told me to follow." She pointed to where he sat among other people in a closed carriage.

"In with you then," said the gentleman gaily. "Stick closer to Big Dorje than his shadow, be secret and careful of your money, and the Holy One will find your dog for you." He laid his hand upon the carriage-door handle.

Momo looked up at him with all the thankfulness of her heart in her eyes. She bowed her head and clasped her hands. and said, "Great and merciful sir, I thank you. May the Blessed One deliver you from all distress! May you be rich and may good health dwell in your house forever!"

The British gentleman answered politely, "It is my good fortune to be chosen as the unworthy agent of the All Merciful." And he added with a smile, "When I was your age I too had a dog that I loved very much."

He opened the door, and leaning toward the people sitting within said, "Make room there for this child, and see, all of you, that she comes to no harm on her journey down to the plains."

The men and women within jumped to their feet, and bowed, their arms full of bundles. They nodded their heads, and smiled and spoke eagerly all together, like a chorus. And the gentleman, looking at Big Dorje, said sternly, "And you, Big Dorje, take especial pains to show the child her way in the city. See that she comes to no harm."

Big Dorje looked like a frightened boy; he bowed awkwardly, and nodded his head, and said, "All right, Burra Lat Sahib, very well, all right, Burra Sahib," in a nervous way.

Then the gentleman turned again to Momo. "Good-by, Momo. Tomorrow morning you will be in Calcutta. May your journey prosper, and you reach success! When you come back this way, stop at the house of Government, and tell the agent of the Lat Sahib who sits there how you have fared."

Momo smiled up at him, and promised to do so. Again she said, "Great mercy!" And she climbed into the carriage, where all the people made way for her as if she had been the daughter of a Maharajah. Then the gentleman stepped back and gave a signal to the station master. With a blast from the train whistle, and a terrible jerk, the train began to move. It threw all the people, who were still standing respectfully before the tall British gentleman, into a heap. They laughed good-naturedly as they disentangled themselves and their bundles, and made room for Momo to sit with them.

"Child," asked one old woman enviously, when all were seated, "how come *you* to be so favored?"

"Oh!" said Momo happily, still in a daze of joy. "He asked me why I cried, and when I said I wanted to get down to Calcutta to get back my dog Pempa, that was stolen from me, he bought me a *tikkut* and brought me here."

The woman looked in amazement round at the others in the carriage. An old man nodded his head wisely as he said, "In a former life the child has gained this merit. Of a surety she is under the protection of the gods."

"Yes," replied Momo simply, "I am. Pempa and I both are under the blessing of the Holy One. It is written in my horoscope that we go to great adventures, and bring fortune to the family. So Dawa has said. And now see the proof—by the grace of God the foreign gentleman gives me a *tikkut* for the plains."

"A miracle indeed, that *he* should trouble himself for the brat," growled Big Dorje. But he looked at Momo with an uneasy respect.

"Why, who *is* he?" asked Momo.

A stir went through the compartment, as all the people heard this question. A pretty young hill woman shook her head till the bangles on her earrings tinkled a silvery chime.

"Was there ever such another?" she asked them all. "She has taken his charity, and does not even know the dispenser of justice!" And then turning to Momo, she said impressively, "That, child, is the Lat Sahib. He is a prince among his own people, and he lives at Gantok like the head of his Government. With him our Maharajah of Sikkhim consults; and even in your own land of Tibet the Lat Sahib is welcome. Yes, alone of all the British, he may go to Lhasa. He speaks your tongue better than you do yourself; and he is the friend of the Dalai Lama and of the Tashi Lama."

A trader from Gyantse, who had listened to these words, nodding his head emphatically, now took the cigarette from his mouth and blew out the smoke thoughtfully as he said, "Of a truth *this* Lat Sahib is a friend to all the hill folk. He knows all our tongues, and our needs; and during very hard times he has helped our holy land of Tibet to preserve the face of dignity and honor, when China would fain have claimed our land as her own, and taken tribute and taxes."

"As she did of old," replied a man of Bhutan. "Is there not

still, near the child's home by the Jelep La pass, the old Chinese customs house, where the Chinese guard of soldiers stayed, and took tribute from all who entered or left your land?"

Big Dorje growled, and the trader from Gyantse nodded. "It is so," he admitted. "There have been evil days in our land, when we have paid China tribute. But the Lat Sahib of the British knows, and all the world beside, that we are a free people; and he uses his strength and that of the British to keep us so. We men of Tibet give him great honor."

Momo nodded eagerly.

"Ah!" she cried. "Was it truly the Lat Sahib? Who among us, even to the little children, does not know the name of the Lat Sahib, and honor him? How often have I heard my father and the muleteers tell of his coming among us! And it was *he*," she murmured in great amazement, "who gave me the *tikkut!* Most truly are we under the blessing of the Enlightened One, Pempa and I." Her face shone with joy. "I *thought* him one who merited great respect."

Big Dorje looked at her sourly. "Aye," he said angrily, "the protection for you, and all your ill luck for me!" He looked around at the others in the carriage. "Is it not a curse that has befallen me," he asked, "that I must stand as the scapegoat for such a child? She goes to Calcutta to look for a dog, forsooth! A *dog,* in that city where the men are as flies upon the sweetmeats in the heat of a July day!"

"Aye, or like all the stars shining in a cloudless sky in the dark of the moon," laughed the trader from Gyantse. "From my heart I pity you, Big Dorje." He looked at Momo. "That city in the plains," he said to her, "is like no other in all the world. It is a swarm of men so thick that beside it the swarming of the bees at a change of hive is as nothing. The houses are like great honeycombs where men are stored layer on layer. The railway station alone—the great hall where the trains run in and rest—this station alone is as big as the monastery at Sera. Here men from all India, and the small hill kingdoms, and from the far north, by Peshawar and even beyond the Khyber Pass, up into Afghan and Baluchistan, and eastward of Kulu, from Ladak—aye, and from far China, over the passes and round by sea, too, they come."

He nodded his head so that his turquoise earring and the feather stuck in his red felt cap shook with his excitement. "Truly," he finished, "the men from all the world are there."

"My father says," added the young hill woman, lifting her arms with a clash of silver bangles, "that the city stretches out over the plain like a thick-set forest of houses and spreads so far that you might walk for many days, and not make the circuit of it."

"And here," said Big Dorje in great disgust, "in this vast jungle of men and houses, we seek a dog! And should that dog not be found, or harm come to this favored one"—he shot a venomous glance at Momo—"then, by the Three Rare Ones, the blame is mine." He looked round the carriage for confirmation of his words, and for sympathy. "The Lat Sahib is not one to forget even so small a trifle as a girl child and her search for a dog. And he will leave word with his agent at the house of Government in Kalimpong to watch for her and for me, on our return. And what think you," he finished uneasily, "will befall *me,* when her search goes amiss, or some ill overtakes the girl?"

Momo looked at him gravely. "Nothing can go amiss," she said, "when the All Powerful One gives support. Then even a mouse may be bold as a lion, soft as a hare, pointed as an arrow."

The whole carriage laughed, and the kindly old hill woman

said peacefully, "The child is right; those under the blessing of the Holy One can come to no harm. And," she added to Big Dorje, "it would be wise for you to wish the child well. 'Whatever happiness is in the world has arisen from a wish for the welfare of others. Whatever misery there is has arisen from indulging in selfishness.'" She finished the old Buddhist proverb in the high drone of a priest, and the whole carriage, listening respectfully to the well-known statement of the Law, fell into silence.

Momo gave herself up to the magic of this swift ride. This train, she thought, is truly a great miracle. It ran round and round the hills, ever dropping downward, dashing about the curves with a screeching of wheels and a grinding of brakes; it rattled and bumped and knocked the people about in their carriage; it poured out a constant cloud of black smoke, and sounded its shrill whistle at the road crossings, and all curves. Every now and then it came to a stop, at a small hill station of the tea estates, and it stopped and started with such violent jerks as to throw them off the narrow bench of the carriage.

"May my life be separated!" gasped the trader from Gyantse, when one unexpected jolt pitched him over into Momo's lap. "To keep seated on this hill train is worse than trying to ride the wild white yak of the Tengri-Nor!"

Momo laughed as she helped him recover his cigarette, pick up his hat, and seat himself again. Although she sat so quietly among these grown folk, her heart was throbbing with the excitement of this mad ride. Every time the train hurtled round a curve, she could look back and see the three cars behind the one in which she rode, and the road they had traveled, lying like a coil of rope slung about the mountainside. And before them she saw their engine puffing smoke, and the road ahead, like more coils of rope twisted round the mountain, down and down, till it was lost in the trees.

They passed through great forests of *sal* and rhododendron and many trees unknown to Momo, past open clearings of small hill farms, and again and again in their curving path they looked down on the foaming waters of the noble Teesta river, rushing, like themselves, down to the plain. At length they screeched round a bend in the road, and came out upon a far-reaching view, where they could look beyond the mountains, and out to a great open space that shimmered in the sun like dusty gold.

"The plains—see, child, there is India," said the pretty hill woman. Momo looked with shining eyes, her heart thumping with excitement.

"It is near," she said, and the woman nodded.

Now the little train had left the mountains behind them, and was running more smoothly over the sloping land that lay between them and the great plain. Here were houses raised on stilts, in among the trees, and as Momo looked at them with wonder, the hill woman said, "This is the *terai,* child, the land between the hills and the plain. Here fevers rise out of the ground with the mists of morning and evening, and there is much malaria. There are also many tigers who live in the jungle. And therefore, to lift them above the fever-bringing mists and the devouring tigers, the people of the *terai* raise their houses upon these high posts."

Momo jumped with excitement. "Oh, how I should like to *see* a tiger!" she cried, craning her head this way and that, to see through the tangled forest. But the hill woman laughed.

"That you will not do," she replied. "My lord the tiger does not come forth to view this train. He sleeps during the heat of the day, and comes out in the early dawn, and again in the cool of evening."

At last the train ran into a kind of great shed, and came to a stop. Then Momo followed the others out, giving up her ticket to the guard as she came out upon the platform. She ran after Big Dorje and the other traders, and stood behind them at the ticket-seller's window. It was so high that she had to stand on tiptoe to look over the ledge, but she put down her silver rupees, which she had clutched tightly in her hand all the time, and said, "One *tikkut* to Calcutta." And the man took up a blue ticket, stamped it, and gave it to her.

"Now you will have three or four hours to wait, child," said the kindly old hill woman, who had been with her all this while. "The night train for Calcutta will come on that track over there. Sit here on the platform to wait for it. I stop here." And she smiled and went away.

Momo looked about for her party of ten traders; and when she saw them sitting in a circle at the end of the station platform she went quietly and sat down near them. Big Dorje scowled at her, but said nothing; and they began their gambling game, shaking the dice in a felt hat, and then turning it down with a thump upon the ground. Momo looked about.

It was hot, the air blew damp and soft against her face, and she sighed with discomfort as she stripped another of her tsampa beads from the string, and sucked it. How she would love a cup of tea! And she had money, too; but had not the Lat Sahib warned her not to open and show her money in an open crowd? And certainly the people clustering about her on the platform were as thick as villagers assembling at the Kargayu monastery for the devil dances. "What matter?" she said to herself philo-sophically. "*Tomorrow morning* I shall be in Calcutta!"

So she watched the scene about her, forgetting herself in the
wonder of it all. Except for themselves, none of these people
wore the heavy, shapeless robes of the Tibetans. Some of the
men were dressed in the white coat and trousers of the English
but most of them were cooler, wrapped in the white cotton dhoti
of the south. Indian ladies too passed by, moving gracefully in
their saris of yellow or green or blue—many colors, all light and
bright and beautiful. A long line of coolies, who now had no
luggage to carry, sat idly in the sunshine, hugging their knees
to their chests. As it dropped near the earth, the sun got bigger
and bigger, and shone with a red-gold light. Momo rose and
walked the length of the platform, and into the open. Behind
her lay the station and the town, all round her stretched this dry
and open land—the great plain of India! "I am *here,* in India!"
she told herself, and still could hardly believe it was really true.
Yet here it lay before her eyes, stretching flat and far to the
horizon, where now the sun, a vast red-gold globe, was sinking.
Everything turned to gold in this last light—the dust that lay
like a haze in the air, the yellow earth—even the station and the
town looked as if they had been dipped in gold.

Turning to the east, she saw the hills rising like a high green
wall, somber blue-green at their base, but shining pink and
purple at their summits, where the sun still shone. Already chill
white mists were creeping up over the sloping land of the *terai,*
blotting out the shapes, so strong and firm, of the mountains.
As she looked at this outermost wall of the high hills, Momo
felt a stab of homesickness for the green and snow-white hills,
for the smell of wood smoke in the cool, clear air, and most of all,
for her home, her jolly father, and her gentle mother.

But the sound of a temple conch blaring solemnly across the
plain brought her another thought. The sun's rim, a golden

bow, slipped below the western earth line. This, the sunset, was the time for prayer. Now, in every monastery in all the hills above her and over all the great plain of Tibet priests were standing, blowing their twenty-foot trumpets, and calling all people to pray. And as in the hills, so in the plains. Another, and yet another conch from Hindu temples farther and farther away sent their notes vibrating across the still plain. Momo prayed.

She looked up to see a Mohammedan, who had come like herself out of the station throng, unfold his little prayer rug. Momo, who had heard her father and the muleteers talk of the followers of the prophet Mohammed, but had never before seen one, watched him gravely. He knelt on the prayer rug, facing toward Mecca, and said his prayers to himself; then he bowed his red fezz to the ground three times, got up, rolled up his prayer rug, and went off.

With the going of the sun a light breeze sprang up, cooling Momo's hot cheeks; and very quickly came the dark. Lamps and electric lights went on in the station, and the waiting people began to stir. There was a noise like thunder on the tracks and a train ran into the station and stopped. Now where were the traders? Momo was in a panic. How had she dared wander away from them, and get lost in the crowd of people pressing now into a thickly wadded mass? She dashed toward the train, in terror lest she lose it.

"Not that way, little fool," said a gruff voice, and Big Dorje jerked her back. "That train has come down from Darjeeling, and brought all these people, who like us go down to Calcutta tonight." Momo smiled up at him and thanked him, but he returned to his gambling game with the gruff warning, "Sit here, and do *you* watch *us*. The prancing steed thinking only of himself falls over the cliff."

In all the noise and confusion of the station, Momo was glad to sit close to the traders and watch the crowd. Many English folk had come on this train from Darjeeling, whole families, fathers and mothers, with little children holding to their hands, and *ayahs* following after, carrying babies. They all went in to the room where food was served, and sat at the tables, eating and drinking. Momo craned her neck to see into the room, where every table was full, and the waiters ran around distractedly trying to keep everyone served and satisfied.

"It is long," she thought ruefully to herself, "since I have had tea, or bread." And she detached another tsampa bead, and sucked it as she looked about. The platform all about her was crowded thick with poor Indians, traveling singly or in families. They sat everywhere in little groups, each man with his possessions tied up in a cloth. Here were many different peoples. There were proud men in the tight-fitting jodhpurs of the warlike Rajputs, burly bearded Sikhs in swaggering turbans, Mohammedan women swathed in the *burkah* in which *purdah* women must travel, hidden from sight in a shapeless white garment with a meshed cloth over the face, or holes cut for vision. It was a never-ending kaleidoscope of form and color. Momo wanted to study every one.

But she was weary from the excitement of the day, and this unusual heat. Her head began to nod, she jerked herself awake, then fell asleep again, and knew nothing until she heard the whirr of heavy wheels on the steel tracks, and was jolted awake by some one shaking her.

"Wake, little fool, or the train will leave you," said Big Dorje. She jumped to her feet and followed him, almost treading upon his red felt boots, in her anxiety not to be separated from him. For now the crowd about her was truly alarming.

Those wealthier folk who had reservations were in no hurry, but sauntered after their servants and their luggage carried on the coolies' heads; but most of the travelers were poor Indians. And they made a wild scramble for the third class carriages, to get themselves seats, and room for their bundles.

Weaving their way among the crush of travelers the sweet-meat-sellers walked up and down, their flat trays of sticky sweets balanced on their heads, shouting their wares. *"Pani-wallah! Pani-wallah!"* shouted the water-vender, sluicing water out of his water jars as he walked, and pouring it accurately into the cupped palms of those who gave him a pice to quench their thirst. A more lordly fellow, pushing his cart of hot tea and scores of tiny red clay cups, shouted on a deeper note: *"Gur-r-rm Chae! Gur-r-rm Chae!"* (Hot tea! Hot tea!) Even in her haste Momo threw a longing glance at the men drinking a last cup of tea, then casting aside the little red clay cup.

A bookstand on wheels came rolling down toward her like the car of Juggernaut. She dodged around it, and slipped between a pair of fruit-sellers, who were balancing trays of green oranges and yellow bananas on their heads, and keeping an eager eye for purchasers as they ran. Through it all, Momo kept before her eyes the red felt cap of Big Dorje. That cap went on and on, down the length of the train. For as usual many more people were traveling than there was any room for; and at length, having walked the whole length of the train, and finding no empty third-class carriage, the traders split up, and forced themselves by twos and threes into tiny compartments already crowded.

Close on Big Dorje's heels Momo climbed into a carriage. She could barely find a toehold within, but clung with determination to her small share of the overcrowded compartment.

"I *am* on this *te-rain* for Calcutta!" she told herself with a thrill of wonder. The carriage was in an uproar. Everyone was shouting at everyone else, pushing and shoving and trying to find themselves more comfortable positions, to hold their many bundles more closely to themselves. But all this yelling, fierce as it sounded, was not ill-natured. When a man slammed shut the carriage door right in Momo's face, and Big Dorje called, "Have a care there! Will you cut off the girl's nose before she is grown?" all the passengers roared with laughter. And then silently, smoothly, almost imperceptibly, the train was in motion, and they glided out of the lights and the uproar of the station, into the darkness of the night.

Momo was standing, wedged between the door and Big Dorje. The carriage was as hot as fire; hot too and steamy was the night air blowing in through the open window, and Momo, in her heavy woolen robe, had never in her life known such torture. "Oh!" she gasped, to Big Dorje. "Here is *Naraka* (hell) itself." But he only smiled maliciously, and replied, "This is the heat of the plains. By day the sun is like a molten ball of gold, and bakes the brain within your skull."

But in spite of her discomfort, Momo was so weary that she fell asleep standing up, with the music of the wheels—Click, click, click, click! Click, click, click, click! *Click,* click, click, click!—beating through her head. Several times the train stopped at country stations, and then there was shouting and noise as people got off and more entered. Each time Momo was wakened by the opening of the door before her, and looked out sleepily at the spacious station, where yellow lamps gleamed. At last she found room on the floor, and slept heavily till morning.

When next she opened her eyes the sun was shining with cloudless brilliance in the blue sky. Everywhere about her stretched the yellow plain, bare and dry now that the season's rice had been cut. Yet, dry as it looked, Momo remembered the words of the learned Lama Pakyung: "And the great plain where the sacred Ganges runs out to the black sea is the province of Bengal—a land so rich that no conqueror of India has stopped till he has made its wealth his own."

The train rolled easily over the level land, past clumps of coconut palms and little villages shaded by spreading mango trees. Each village had its own water supply—a square *tank* (pool), where people were bathing. Women too were there washing clothes, or filling and carrying off on their heads great copper jars of water for their households. Momo looked in wonder at their great use of water, for in her cold land people almost never bathed, and did not often wash. She stared too at the houses, roofed with a thick thatch of rice straw that rose in a graceful dome above the walls.

"Why do they make the roofs like that?" she wondered out loud, and Big Dorje, who was growing almost kind, looked out and said, "To carry the heavy monsoon rains away from the walls, which are made of dried mud." Momo, happy to have him so pleasant, smiled up at him, and then exclaimed, "O! See!" A flock of brilliant green parakeets swooped out of the sky and perched on the telegraph wire before her.

The train ran and stopped; ran on and stopped, then ran again—and now through a place where great houses stood close together and roads ran everywhere, all of them filled with people. While Momo gazed, thinking with a shiver of joy, "This is Calcutta!" the train ran into a great sunless place and stopped. Big Dorje opened the door and was the first man out, saying to Momo as he went, "Follow. Here is Sealdah Station." And close upon his heels Momo sprang after him.

The platform was a thick jam of people: all those who were stepping off the train, and those who had come to meet them, were struggling to meet, to move, to make their way through the crowd. Everywhere coolies darted like a flock of hungry crows, pouncing upon luggage, and piling it piece after piece on top of their heads. Voices went up in a roar to the iron girders of the metal ceiling—friends greeting, mothers screaming shrilly at their children to keep together, coolies shouting for hire, and travelers shouting directions to coolies.

And in this solid river of people slowly flowing toward the gate, Big Dorje and the traders and little Momo moved, gave up their tickets, and came out into a vast stone-floored room, peopled with second- and third-class travelers patiently awaiting their trains. Through this crowd Big Dorje moved expertly, circling families who sat huddled about their boxes and bundles, stepping carelessly over the many men who lay like white-swathed mummies fast asleep, giving respectful distance to a high-born Mohammedan lady in a red and glittering burkah who stood surrounded by her servants and her luggage—a dozen lacquered trunks, wicker baskets, even a bird cage.

Then the ten traders, with Momo close at their heels, passed out under a great arch and into an open road. But what a road! Here was a space huge as the courtyard at the Kargayu monastery, and it was a sea of traffic. Momo gasped. While she was staring dizzily, a car rolled past them almost over her very feet. With a little scream she leaped back upon the pavement.

But the ten traders pushed out stolidly into this moving jam and conquering her fear, if not losing it, Momo followed. Now she could see that there were waves of direction in this sea of traffic. In the center of the space, far out beyond the station, a man in white stood under a big umbrella. When he raised his arm and blew sharply upon a whistle, one wave of traffic streamed into the station, and the outbound travelers, she and the ten traders among them, stood still. With the next signal the outbound traffic swept forward, and the incoming traffic halted. But because of the crush, progress was very slow.

Big Dorje turned and shouted to her above the roar. "We men take the bus to the shop of Wing Fong the Chinese, where all our Tibetan folk in Calcutta go. Have you money for the bus?"

Then in the uproar, confused by the jostling crush of people, frightened at the possibility of getting separated from the traders, her one thought Pempa and Big Dorje as a guide to him, Momo forgot the warning of the Lat Sahib.

"Yes. Oh, yes, I have the money," she shouted back. She did not see the boy beside her, fixing a quick and greedy eye upon her. Without any caution or concealment she pulled out her red scarf and began to untie the knots that held her money fast.

"Good!" replied Big Dorje. "Follow closely, for we go now to the bus." He turned.

Again the policeman blew his whistle. Now the crowd about her surged forward, the traders with it, Momo following, her eyes intently fixed on Big Dorje's red cap. She saw no one, nothing else; she did not observe the boy close at her side, his furtive glancing at her red scarf. Suddenly his foot shot out, his hand snatched at the scarf. Momo tripped over the outstretched foot and fell heavily, striking her head against the cobbled road.

The wave of traffic still swept on. As if she had been a log of wood men stepped over and around her, not stopping, not helping, not even noticing that she had fallen. Momo scrambled to her feet, holding her aching head, searching frantically for Big Dorje's red cap. Gone! In those few seconds the traders had vanished. The bus had swallowed them up and carried them off.

And—Mother Tara!—her hands were empty. The red scarf was gone.

VII. LOTUS BLOSSOM'S PLAN

"Chor! Chor!" (Thief! Thief!)

At once Momo shouted the cry—which once sounded in a bazaar is picked up by a thousand throats, and sends all hearers scurrying to help find the thief. But here was no leisurely bazaar, delighted to spice the daily business of buying and selling with the drama of hunting thieves. No one heard her. Like a mighty river in flood tide the crowd pushed on, hearing nothing, seeing nothing, stopping only for the policeman's whistle, carrying everything, herself included, in its rush. "As if," Momo thought bitterly, "I were a dried stick on the Chumbi river when the spring thaws carry off the snows of winter."

With a last desperate hope, she looked searchingly at all those about her; but all the men walked empty-handed, easily. The thief must by now have got far away. "As well seek through a raging snowstorm for the tracks of yesterday's caravan," Momo muttered to herself.

Everything that she had been warned of had now happened. She thought of the words of the kind woman at the tea shop in Lingtu: "You will come to a land where no one will understand what you say." All about her the crowd was shouting excitedly, and whether it was Bengali or Hindi or Urdu, Momo did not know. She did not even know Hindustani, that mixture of the Hindu and the Mohammedan languages, by which all the peoples of north India can understand each other.

And the warning of the Lat Sahib: "Do not show your money, for in Calcutta there are many quick and clever thieves." How could she have been so forgetful of these words? Especially at this great station, where simple hill folk would be first coming into the bewildering city—especially there, thieves would find it easy to fleece them unawares. Now that it was too late, Momo knew how easily the thieves got their loot. She was angry, furiously angry—angry at the thief and angry at herself.

"O foolish and heedless one, whom not even the utmost care of the Holy One can protect!" she muttered to herself. "Take now the results of your own folly!" And she let herself be carried along in this flood of men, stopping and starting at the policeman's whistle, pushing out into the traffic that filled Lower Circular Road.

But once she was away from the station the crowds melted, and she found herself in the comparative quiet of the day's beginning. Merchants were taking down the wooden shutters from their shops, and arranging their goods within. Herdsmen

were rounding up the cows from their homes in the courtyards
of city houses, and driving them out through the streets to the
open grass of the Maidan. Few people yet walked the streets,
and not knowing what else to do, Momo followed the road. It
was a wide one, lined on both sides by high houses, and every
house had on its ground floor a shop.

Momo looked about her, and now that her anger had died
away, she felt small and very much alone. A feeling of dismay,
even the beginning of fear, began to come over her. Here were
the great houses where men were stored layer on layer, and the
streets that stretched out endlessly—and here too somewhere
was Pempa. But where? And how, now that she had lost the
traders, could she ever find him? Her mind was confused, she
grew more and more frightened, and since she could not think,
she began to hurry. The farther she went the more crowded the
street became, as the day's work got under way. Men, talking
excitedly and thinking only of their own business, pushed her
about on the pavement. The street too was noisy from the streetcars clanging their bells at the slow creaking lines of bullock
carts.

"O Tara, Mother of Mercy!" she thought desperately.
"Stay with me now! Lead me, unworthy as I am, to Pempa!"
But even this prayer did not lift the fear that clutched at her
heart, and the cloud that numbed her mind. Confused and
helpless, she wandered on until the street ended at a crossroad
in a great open space. Open, but not empty. For here the traffic
became a dense and solid jam.

Momo stood on the pavement at the brink of this swirling
whirlpool, and looked fearfully about. What to do? Which way
to turn? While she hesitated, the crowd decided for her. It
picked her up and swept her in its current across the great open

space, before the traffic policeman's umbrella, over the tracks of the streetcars, and into the footpath of a wide bridge spanning a mighty river.

All the middle section of this bridge was a wide road choked with vehicles. Streetcars running on tracks and clanging their bells; busses lacquered gold or silver, with people looking out of all the windows; motor cars; closed carriages like square boxes, drawn by little horses and shutting away the face of some Indian lady from the world; rickshaws pulled by sweating coolies; bullock carts laden with rice or jute: four and five abreast, coming or going, they streamed in contrary currents. On each side were broad paths for foot passengers—men walking, coolies swaying as they jog-trotted along, cleverly balancing their sacks of rice upon their heads. It was a moving bridge of men, most marvelous to see. Every man and every carriage in the city must be there, Momo thought. And this bridge spanned a river so vast that Momo looked down on it in awe.

"Is this the sacred Ganges?" she murmured to herself. Her face clouded. "But it is full of mud! Not clear and foaming like our little Chumbi river." She looked with distaste at the heavy yellow water. But even as she looked the words of the learned Lama Pakyung, when he lay in their home recovering of an illness, came back to her.

"That branch of the many-mouthed sacred Ganges which flows through Calcutta," he had said, "men call the Hoogli. And like all the mouths of holy Mother Ganges it is yellow as gold with precious silt. For Mother Ganges plays like a willful child. All along her course she tears at the land with ravening mouth, snatching away the rich soil to lay it like a golden blanket over the rice fields of lower Bengal.

"And that," he had added thoughtfully, "is both a blessing

and a curse. For the silt that makes the fields so fertile also dams the river currents; it is always changing the course of the great birdlike ships that sail into Calcutta from the far quarters of the world. Aye!" He had raised on one elbow to make his words more strong. "It is truth, my own eyes have seen—great islands of that silt spring up overnight in mid-river, where before there was no solid land. And men row out to such isles and plant and raise there both paddy and jute. But that is only a small part of holy Mother Ganges' magic." And he had fallen silent, meditating on the wonders of this holy stream, which all men of India hold in reverence.

So Momo, remembering, looked down upon that vast flood, half expecting to see islands rise up in midstream. But the water rolled swiftly, steadily down to the sea, and the wind and the currents rippled its surface into waves which reflected the sunlight like mirrors, constantly changing. Dancing up and down on these waves were shoals of little black country boats. Downstream a cluster of them looked like children's slippers, lined up at the river bank. Farther down, great ships were lying side by side in the stream, tied securely fore and aft to black buoys like giant drums.

"*Lah-se!*" Momo murmured. "Those are surely the birdlike ships, great as the clouds at dawn, that sail over the black waters from the far quarters of the world." How large this world, how full of wonders! And best and most joyous of wonders, she, Momo, was here, here in Calcutta—and here was Pempa!

"Pempa! O Pempa!" she thought longingly. "Where are you? *I am coming!*" And suddenly her heart was light as a feather; she did not care about the loss of her money, or the disappearance of the ten traders. She was not afraid of this great city, or the crowds of people. She moved along with them, sure of one thing. Pempa was *here,* and she would find him. Perhaps she might even see him—pass him on the road, she thought, as she saw a yellow pi-dog running between the bullock carts. Then she shook her head. "No, no!" she told herself proudly. "Pempa will be sitting in the house of princes, not running the streets like a homeless stray."

But how to find that prince's house? By this time Momo was drawing near the end of the great bridge. Here another policeman stood in the middle of the way, controlling the flow of traffic, most of which was trying to turn to the left, to enter a vast building. Momo stayed well away from the center of the traffic this time, fearing to be swept into this great building; she moved straight forward, off the bridge, and out into a crowded, noisy, and dirty road. On one side were the walls surrounding that huge building and on the other houses and shops. Now, in spite of the noise and the confusion of the traffic, Momo felt alert and unafraid.

"The shop of Wing Fong the Chinese, where all men of Tibet who are in Calcutta go!" Big Dorje's words echoed in her mind. There she must go to get news of Pempa's whereabouts. But how to find that shop? Every house in this city seemed to be a shop, she thought, as she walked and looked. The whole city must be a bazaar!

No, here, just here, the solid line of houses was broken. In a tiny courtyard a little temple stood apart, and set back from the street. Its gates were open, and on a sudden impulse Momo walked in and sat down on the temple steps. Here it was peaceful, and the noise of the street was a more distant roar. "Oof! How hot, this city!" she said, and wiped the streaming sweat from her face. Suddenly hungry, she began sucking a bit of tsampa while she sat, confidently waiting for her next direction.

Before long she heard voices behind her, and jumping up, made way for two men who were coming down the steps from the temple. Both were dressed in the orange robe of the monk, and Momo quickly stuck out her tongue and stood aside respectfully for them to pass. The older one smiled and moved on quietly. But even as Momo stared at the younger man who followed, thinking, "He looks like one of us," the young priest paused and spoke.

"O daughter of the hills!" he said. "What are you doing here, so far from the white snow mountains and the great plains?" And—Oh, joy!—he spoke in her own tongue.

"O holy one! May you live long!" Momo cried happily. "I seek my dog Pempa. But first I must find the shop of Wing Fong the Chinese where all the men of Tibet who come to this city go. Can you tell me the way?"

The lad nodded his close-cropped head, and his black eyes sparkled. "Have I not myself eaten the bread of his charity?" he replied. "When first I came wandering out of the hills seeking work, before I found this my teacher and served him first as servant and now as disciple, Wing Fong gained merit by giving this unworthy one both food and shelter." He smiled down at her. "Most surely I can tell you the way there."

Momo clasped her hands and cried, "Thank you, thank you! That is great kindness, never to be forgotten."

"Then follow me," replied the young lad. "We go your way." And with long strides he overtook his teacher, who had not once looked back, but was moving serenely along the street. Momo followed the two, close on their heels, determined not to lose sight of these heaven-sent guides.

"We are in Howrah now," said the young disciple, turning

to Momo. "And there is the Howrah Station." He pointed to the great enclosed building where the crush of traffic was worse. "Before reaching Calcutta we must cross the river by this Howrah bridge."

Momo nodded, realizing how far she had gone out of her way in her ignorance. But she walked again with pleasure over that wondrous bridge, gazing at the mighty river, and never losing her place behind the two orange-clad monks. When they had left the bridge its vast crowds and traffic spread out and trickled away into the different streets, becoming part of the busy life of Calcutta. The two priests walked swiftly down the crowded street, block after block, while Momo, now that she felt free of fear, looked about and marveled at the number of people and houses. She longed to stop for only a moment to see the goldsmiths' shops, where silver bracelets and anklets and earrings were for sale; and she looked hungrily at the food shops, where sweetmeats boiled over a charcoal fire, or men stood deftly turning thick, white *chappatis* on a round clay oven. How good it smelled, this hot bread! But the two priests ahead of her strode on, never glancing to right or left, telling their prayers on rosaries as they walked. They stopped at last, where a crossroad took a winding course through the city.

"Here we must leave you," said the young priest, turning to Momo with his flashing smile. "But from here you cannot miss the shop of Wing Fong the Chinese. Walk straight ahead to the next street, and cross it; walk to a second street, and cross it; walk to a third cross street, turn left and at the end of two blocks you come to the road end. There, on your right, the last house in the street is the shop of Wing Fong the Chinese."

"Walk to the first street, and cross; to the second street, and cross; walk to the third cross street, turn left and at the end of two blocks I come to the road end. And there on my right is the shop of Wing Fong the Chinese," Momo repeated parrot-like.

"Yes, that is right," the young priest nodded. "Now when you enter, you will see first a counter with rows of little sausages and dried mushrooms hanging over it; and in the room there are tables where Chinese men sit drinking tea. Pass by the counter and pass by the tables where the men drink tea, and at the far corner of the room you will come to a flight of stairs that goes straight up the side of the wall. Climb these stairs. Pass a door on your left where the children of Wing Fong play, and go out into a long room that overlooks the street. There is the shop for the Tibetans, and there you will find word of your Pempa."

Momo bent her head, then looked up with great thankfulness at the two orange-clad monks.

"O guide of the poor! Givers of wisdom! May you reap infinite bliss in the land of the blessed!" she said. They both smiled, the young lad joyously, the old monk tenderly, and blessed her. Then they turned and strode away, not looking to right nor to left, murmuring their prayers as they went.

Momo walked as she was told: to the next street, and crossed; to the second street, and crossed; to the third street, and turned left. Ahead of her she saw houses like a barrier; and when she had walked two blocks, she had come to the road end.

"And here, at the corner, is the shop of Wing Fong the Chinese!" she repeated triumphantly to herself.

So she went in and saw before her the counter where little sausages and dried mushrooms hung from strings above the counter; passed the tables where Chinese men sat drinking tea; found the little flight of stairs in the far corner, and climbed straight up the side of the wall. Then she peeped through an open door on her left, where two girls in Chinese blue coats and trousers were playing with a little boy. She passed them by, and came out into a big room, whose windows overlooked the street below.

Here there were rows and rows of gay colored china dishes on counters against the walls, and on long tables set out in the middle of the room. And here, at a fine table of Chinese black-wood, sat the ten traders, drinking tea! Momo stared at them, the traders stared at her, astonished. And at the look of stupefied amazement and then of relief, that came over Big Dorje's face, Momo laughed aloud. Finally he shook his head and remarked to his fellows, "May I die before sunset! Of a certainty this brat is under the protection of the Blessed One." And of Momo he asked, "How came you here?"

She replied simply, "A thief knocked me down and stole my money. So I started to walk; and two priests showed me the way. Where is Wing Fong the shopkeeper?"

They nodded toward a far corner of the room. There two prosperous Tibetan traders had set down the silver base and cover of their tea cups, and were looking for china bowls to fit. A slender Chinese brought out one bowl after another of fine white porcelain, gaily painted with dragons or little black-haired Chinese. Momo came and stood near them, watching quietly until at last the two buyers, still not having found exactly the bowls they wanted for their precious tea, began looking for themselves among the high piles along the counters. Then the Chinese turned and smiled at her.

Momo greeted him, and spoke, and her voice trembled with excitement.

"O protector of the poor! O friend of all men from the high

hills! I seek five traders with two dogs, one black, and one a red-gold Lhasa terrier. Have you seen such men?"

The Chinese's face was little and round, and it broke into a wide smile as he looked at her.

"Yes, yes," he nodded. "I have seen, I have seen. Two, three days back they came, and did much business. Yesterday they go away back home."

Momo's heart jumped into her mouth. "But the dog," she said breathlessly. "The golden Lhasa terrier! Where is he?"

The Chinese looked at her with his black eyes and his whole face screwed up in surprise.

"Oh, yes," he said finally. "That yellow dog. I remember him. Yes, they have taken him to be sold. And they did sell."

"Where, where?" screamed Momo. "That's *my* dog—my dog Pempa!"

"Ah! Ah!" murmured the little Chinese, shaking his head sorrowfully at her. "I am sorry, but now he is sold away, your dog."

"Oh, where? To whom?" cried Momo. "I must get him back. I want him. My Pempa!" And suddenly she burst out crying, as if her heart would break.

"Ah-h-h! Ah-h-h!" said the two daughters of Wing Fong, who had seen Momo pass by, and now came running out into the shop with their little brother to look at her. They stood before her.

"Why do you cry, Tibetan girl?" asked Lotus Blossom, the older of the two girls. And Momo, opening her eyes to look at them, sobbed, "My dog, Pempa! My golden Lhasa terrier! They stole him out of my house, and—" she shut her eyes again and sobbed—"they *sold* him!"

The two little Chinese girls shook their heads. "Ah, ah!"

they said in sympathy. Then Lotus Blossom turned to her father, and asked, "To whom did they sell him, honorable father?" Wing Fong looked uncomfortable, as if he did not want to talk about it. But the children pressed him.

"To whom? Where *is* he?" insisted Momo, stopping her sobbing for a moment.

Wing Fong, who was very kindhearted, and loved children, looked more and more uncomfortable. Finally he said to Momo, "Go home, little girl."

"I will not—not until I get my Pempa back!" interrupted Momo passionately.

Wing Fong spread out his hands hopelessly. "But you cannot get him back. You *cannot!*"

"*Why* not?" asked Momo obstinately. "I have come all the way down from the top of the Jelep La pass to Calcutta to find him, and I am not going back until I do get him."

"Good! That is right," said Lotus Blossom decidedly. And little White Jade and her brother, Gift of Heaven, both nodded their heads and echoed, "Good! Good!"

"Where have they taken him, Father?" asked Lotus Blossom again. "She must find him."

Wing Fong looked very unhappy. "But you cannot get your dog back again," he said, "even if I tell you where he is gone."

"Why not?" cried Momo, indignantly, and Lotus Blossom, White Jade, and little Gift of Heaven each in turn echoed her question.

"Why not?"

"Why not?"

"Why not?"

Poor Wing Fong looked about as if he wanted to run away from these tormenting children, but Lotus Blossom caught his hand and coaxed him softly, "Tell us, honorable father, where they have taken the dog."

And very reluctantly he replied, "A great English lady has paid much money for him, and the trader has taken the silver and gone back with it to Tibet. You should have waited there in your home," he added, to Momo. "Then your father and your mother might have made him give you back the silver rupees he has taken for your dog. Now you cannot get the dog back. Even if that great English lady would kindly return him to you, where would you get the money to give to her?"

Momo had stopped crying to listen breathlessly to him, but when she understood what he had said, she started screaming again. Lotus Blossom began to cry with her in sympathy. Little White Jade and Gift of Heaven opened their mouths wide, and howled too.

"Oh! Oh! Children! Like dogs tied on the housetop, barking at and trying to bite the stars of heaven, why do you disturb our peace?" cried the two traders who were looking for fine tea cups. They stopped their search to scowl at the children, and said, "Stop them at once, Wing Fong."

"Yes, stop them! Quiet!" said the ten traders from their table in the middle of the room, turning to look at Momo, and growling like surly mastiffs who see a stranger nearing their home.

Now Wing Fong expected to do profitable business with the two rich traders, and he was giving the ten traders tea—not the thin Chinese tea, but their own thick, buttered Tibetan tea ---to put them in good humor before starting to trade with him. So he very particularly did not want to make them angry. He waved his arms about and tried to stop the children's screams.

"Be quiet, all of you! What do you want? What can *I* do?"

Lotus Blossom, who was very quick and clever, looked up at him slyly out of her slanting black eyes.

"Only tell us where they took the dog, Father," she said softly, "and then Momo can go there to see for herself what can be done."

Momo stopped crying and looked at him. White Jade and Gift of Heaven too stopped suddenly, their mouths still wide open and stared at him. Wing Fong wrinkled his forehead, and rubbed his hands together, and looked most unhappy.

"This is a hard thing you ask," he replied. "They are very great people, and do much costly business with me."

"But it can't hurt *you*," said Momo. "He's *my* dog."

"Well!" said Wing Fong. And to himself he thought, "Let her go. The child will never be allowed within the house." And comforted by this thought, he spoke.

"Hear then the story of your dog, little Momo." All four children stood before him in a circle, breathless with excitement.

"Last year," he began, "when Nema Doorg, the Tibetan wool trader, was in my shop, he had with him that black dog of which you spoke. And also in my shop was the Paton Lady Memsahib, the wife of the Military Secretary to the Governor of Bengal. She is a very great lady—next to head of Government, you see. She buys many things from me here; and she brings here many other Memsahibs—Memsahibs living in Calcutta, and many who come out from England to see India. They all do much business with me. So you see," he threw an appealing look at his Lotus Blossom, who was quite old enough to understand the importance of trade, "I do not want to make the Paton Lady Memsahib angry at me."

"No, no," said Lotus Blossom firmly. "She will not be angry. Go on."

"Yes, go on," echoed Momo, and White Jade and Gift of Heaven piped in their high voices. "Yes, go on! Go on!"

Wing Fong, still dubious, sighed and took up his story.

"The Paton Lady Memsahib looked at the black dog, and said to me, 'Wing Fong, ask that Tibetan if he knows a good Lhasa terrier when he sees one. That one of his is not pure bred.'

"So I asked Nema Doorg, and he said he did know a good one when he saw it.

"Then the Paton Lady Memsahib said, 'Then tell him if he will bring me a really good Lhasa terrier the next time he comes down to Calcutta—a well-bred dog, and in good condition, mind you—I will pay him one hundred rupees for it. If it is a *really* good dog.'"

"Oh!" breathed Lotus Blossom, widening her eyes in astonishment at this great sum of money. She looked at Momo with a new respect. "That is *much* money—your dog is very, very costly."

"Yes, of course," said Momo impatiently. "Go on, Wing Fong." And Wing Fong, still reluctant, continued.

"Then this year when Nema Doorg came in, he said, 'How shall I find that Memsahib who wants the terrier? For I have brought one down to her. And an evil-tempered beast it is, too,' he added. 'But it is a good one, and will surely fetch the hundred rupees she promised me.'"

Momo, who would not have sold Pempa for all the silver in the world, ground her teeth, and looked furiously angry.

"And then?" she said.

Wing Fong shrugged his shoulders. "Well then, I gave him the address, and he went, and the Paton Lady Memsahib took the dog and gave him the money, and now he has gone back to Tibet." He stopped and looked at the four somber children before him, and shook his head and rubbed his hands together helplessly.

"I did not know the dog was stolen," he said to Momo. "I am so very sorry. But now there is nothing to do. Go home, little daughter, and your father will get you another dog."

Momo's face darkened with anger to hear herself put off again with that old promise; but before she could speak, Lotus Blossom frowned at her father and said firmly, "Momo is going straight to the house of the Military Secretary Sahib, and if you won't tell her how to get there, I will!"

"It is a long, long way, through many twisting streets," said Wing Fong, suddenly frightened again at the thought that he might anger Lady Paton, and lose all her fine trade.

"Oh, no matter how far it is," said Momo eagerly. "Haven't I walked all the way out of the high snow mountains of Tibet to find him?"

"No need to walk," said Lotus Blossom decidedly. "My honorable father will send you in a rickshaw. Yes you will, Father," she added as he started to protest. "Momo will ride in our own rickshaw. You did not know the dog was stolen when you sent Nema Doorg there. Momo will explain that. Those English are very straight. For your kind act in helping Momo you will gain merit from the Paton Lady Memsahib as well as from heaven."

And so, to get rid of the children, and be free to go back to his business with the Tibetan traders, Wing Fong gave his consent. Momo saluted him politely, and smiled joyously.

"Great thanks," she said. "May you be rich! May no sickness come to you or yours! May you live long!" And all three of his own children bowed before him, and said, "We thank you, honorable father."

Then Lotus Blossom took Momo by the hand, and ran out of the shop. White Jade and Gift of Heaven ran after them. They pattered down the steps, through the tea room, past the counter where the little sausages hung, and out into the street. There Lotus Blossom clapped her hands and called.

"Sita-ram! O Sita-ram!"

After some time a coolie came around the corner of the house and asked, "What is it?"

"Bring the rickshaw here—my father's orders," said Lotus Blossom, and when he had brought it, and put down the shafts on the ground, Lotus Blossom said, "Climb in, Momo. See, take hold this way," and she helped Momo to seat herself. Then she turned to the rickshaw coolie.

"Sita-ram, take this girl quickly to the house of the Military Secretary of the Governor Sahib. You know the house. So many times you carry parcels there for my father. And don't come back," she added, "till you can tell me whether Momo sees the Burra Memsahib or not."

"*A-accha!*" (All right!) said Sita-ram, smiling at the children. He stepped between the shafts and lifted the rickshaw. Momo, who had been hanging to the handrails, gasped as she and the carriage were suddenly lifted, and the wheels began to roll. The three little Chinese children laughed at her astonishment. Then they waved to her, and cried, "Good-by, Momo! Good luck! May you get back your dog!"

Not daring to let go her grasp of the handrails, Momo sat very stiffly. But she smiled and nodded at them, and tried to show how full her heart was of thankfulness.

"Oh, thank you! Thank you! Good-by," she called, as Sita-ram, having turned the rickshaw, carried her down the street at a nimble jog-trot.

VIII. FULFILLMENT OF THE PROPHECY:
GOOD FORTUNE

Such excitement! Momo's heart was pounding at her ribs, and she quivered all over at the thought, Pempa! *At last I am coming to you!* She gave not a thought to the money that had been paid for him, nor to whether she now had a right to him. Pempa was *hers*. She knew at last where he was, and she was traveling to him in state, rolling through the huge city in this fine rickshaw.

Oh, Pempa, she thought laughingly, you are in the house of Government, but I am coming to you, carried like a lady. She looked with pleasure at the blue cushioned seat and the hood to protect the rider from sun or rain. How very strange it felt merely to sit above those turning wheels, and bowl gently down the street! And to watch the trotting legs of the rickshaw man before her in the shafts! Since she had grown too big to be lifted astride her father's shoulder or her mother's hip, Momo had never been carried by anything but her own strong legs. She laughed aloud with pleasure at this strange sensation, and the coolie turning, grinned at her and called to her cheerfully, *"Tik hai, baccha!"* (All right, little girl!)

From this height too everything looked different than from the street level. She could see farther, and more, and even looked down on the children playing in the street. How many houses, and more people—and how unlike anything she had ever seen! Momo stared wide-eyed, with such excitement and such joy in her heart at the thought that she was going at last to fetch Pempa back, that all she saw was burned into her mind. As long as she lived Momo would remember that rickshaw ride through the twisting Calcutta streets, and the people who crowded them.

At first these streets were so narrow that there was room for one vehicle only. Sita-ram the coolie clanged his bell constantly as he jogged along, and shouted too to get the swarming children off the road. Impudent little Bengali boys darted under the very wheels of the rickshaw, and seemed to make a game of moving just before the coolie ran them down. The pavement was only about a foot wide, so that when fat little Chinese babies, in the care of older sisters, toddled suddenly out from the houses they were at once in the street. Momo held her breath for fear they would be run over.

Suddenly they were face to face with a motor car. It had turned a corner, and was moving slowly along this street, its mudguards almost scraping the curbstones. Inside they could see the driver, in a splendid crisp white turban, and in the back seat a British lady, riding alone. Momo gazed terrified into the broad black nose and great glass eyes of the motor, and wanted to spring for safety into the nearest house. But Sita-ram the coolie had no fear. He let the shafts of the rickshaw come to rest at arm's length, and planting his legs far apart, held his ground. They were so close to the great car, purring like a tiger, that they felt its hot breath on their cheeks. The driver leaned out and shouted impatiently at them.

"O coolie! Back! Go back, and let me pass!"

"O driver!" shouted Sita-ram in reply. "*I* am the one to go forward. Back! Out of my way!"

"Does my lord the tiger turn aside for the crawling ant?" snorted the driver in great contempt. Sita-ram threw back his head and scowled. He had the finest rickshaw and the best master in Calcutta, and he was not ashamed to be a rickshaw man.

"O senseless one! Croaking like a bloated bull frog!" he called. "The mud of your village is still thick upon your head if you do not know that in this city we men have rules of traffic. *I* have the right of way. Go back!"

The driver shook his white turban and his arm with rage, and poured abuse over Sita-ram like a wave. The coolie was not disturbed; he loved such furious word battles, and was ready to stand cursing in his shafts until sundown. Back and forth the volleys of invective flew, as both men warmed to the game of heaping abuse upon the other.

"Owl! Son of a nameless father, whose mother had no nose!" Sita-ram finished one long withering attack, and paused to draw breath for the next. His tongue was just getting well loosened, his brain fertile in abuse. But the English lady leaned forward and spoke urgently to her driver, and very reluctantly. hurling ill names at Sita-ram all the while, he backed his car round the corner. Sita-ram lifted the shafts and trotted cheerfully on, tossing one final blistering remark to the driver as he left. And Momo breathed a sigh of deep relief.

She was glad when they came out of these narrow twisted streets where the Chinese people in Calcutta lived; then for block after block they passed tall houses, each with its shop, and here and there an open bazaar. The streets were all crowded thick with men and children walking, buying, selling or just sitting or standing idly about. Rounding a corner, Sita-ram came out upon a busy street where streetcars ran, and the domes of a big Mohammedan mosque rose at the intersection corner. From here on he drew the rickshaw through wider, quieter streets of large European shops and office buildings, crossed one very broad street, and ran beside a fine circular park, enclosed by a high fence of iron railings.

Its great gates were thrown open, and two Indian soldiers stood there on guard, like bronze statues. Peering down the long avenue within, Momo saw a big white building, crowned with a dome, and thought to herself, "Ah! Here is the palace of the Burra Lat Sahib." And so it was. Turning into the street that ran up and ended just at the gates of the Governor's palace, Sita-ram drew up with a flourish before a stately house on the corner. Momo jumped lightly down.

Two guards stopped her at the curb. They were Gurkhas, men from the hills, who look very small and wiry, but are fierce fighters. They were so much of a size and looked so much alike that they might have been twins. And very proud they were of themselves and their duty of guarding the house of the Military

Secretary, and of their white uniforms, and above all, of the red band, the symbol of Government men, which they wore twisted around their turbans. They looked scornfully at this small Tibetan girl in her dark wool robe.

"O, *durwans!*" cried Sita-ram. "Here is a child from the hills, who knows nothing, and speaks no tongue but that of the *Bhotiyas* (Tibetans). She has come from the shop of Wing Fong the Chinese to see the Burra Memsahib, Paton Lady Memsahib." He set down the shafts of his rickshaw and lounged at ease, waiting curiously to see what would happen. The two guards shouted at him angrily.

"Go away! *Jungly wallah!* (Stupid country fellow!) Is this a common rickshaw stand where all the scum of the city may hire themselves a ride? *Jao!* Go away!" And they brandished their sticks at him fiercely. In a matter-of-fact way, for this was no more than he had expected, Sita-ram picked up the shafts and moved off, to stop again and watch from a post at the corner. And as he went he shouted at them in amiable contempt.

"Hah! Durwans! Why are all the *paharis* (men of the hills) durwans and soldiers of the regiment? Because they have pumpkins for heads!" To this the durwans, remembering the dignity of their position, made no reply. They stared at Momo, who had stepped upon the pavement and stood before them, trying to pass.

"Halt! No beggars are allowed here," said one of the guards, who spoke her tongue. Both men brandished their sticks before her nose, and edged her off the pavement. But Momo was not afraid of them, and stood her ground. To herself she thought, "Pempa is *inside that house!*" and the thought gave her the courage of a tiger. She spoke politely but firmly.

"I am not a beggar. I am Momo, and I have come down from

the top of the Jelep La pass over the boundaries of Bhotiyal to see the—" she hesitated, forgetting the strange English name. "the Memsahib who lives here, who is next to head of Government."

The two durwans studied her with bright, black eyes, keen as a crow's, and Gopal, who understood her words, repeated them for his fellow. He spoke in a high falsetto, mimicking her child's voice, and then both durwans, who were merry little fellows, threw back their heads and laughed.

"Ho! Ho! Ho! She wants to see the Burra Memsahib," they said again. "Ho! Ho! Ho!" They laughed and laughed until Momo flushed with anger.

"Yes," she said with determination. "I have come to see her, and I will not leave here until I *do* see her." Struck by the tone of her voice, the durwans stopped laughing, and stared again at her.

"What does she want, Gopal?" asked Rama of his fellow.

"Why do you want to see our Burra Memsahib, child?" repeated Gopal.

"I want my dog Pempa," said Momo, her lips trembling as she spoke the beloved name. "They stole him and brought him here."

The two durwans considered this information, shaking their heads and pursing up their mouths. Being kindly men, and like all Indians tenderly indulgent to children, they were sorry for the disappointment she must feel. Softly, comfortingly, therefore, Gopal spoke.

"We are sorry, little girl, but you must go home. You cannot get your dog back. Our Burra Memsahib has paid much money —oh, a fortune she has paid!—for this dog."

The durwans knew to a pice how much had been paid for the

dog, since they had exacted a fee from Nema Doorg for graciously permitting him entrance into the house, when he had come to deliver Pempa to Lady Paton. It was not at all a bad thing to be a doorkeeper and to have the power to admit or turn away those who came to speak with Lord or Lady Paton. Many kinds of Indians came every day, seeking many different kinds of favors. None ever got past these sturdy durwans without slipping a coin into their hands. Of course this was bribery, and strictly forbidden by the British officials of Government; but it was also the age-old custom of India, and in a mere three hundred years of occupation, the British had not been able to make the Indians change their habit of greasing the palm of doorkeepers who stood between themselves and those they wished to see. Gopal and Rama had taken their profit from this sale when the money for Pempa had been paid to Nema Doorg, and that ended the matter.

"It is finished, child," Gopal concluded. "Your dog is sold. You must go home."

"But he is *mine*," protested Momo. No matter how often people told her Pempa had been sold, she still could not believe anything but that he was hers. As long as he lived Pempa belonged to her, and she *would* have him. The two durwans, however, were beginning to weary of this stupid little hill girl, who had no money to slip into their hands, and no sense to understand a clear sale.

"Go away, girl," said Gopal impatiently. "You are as stupid as an owl. Our Burra Memsahib has *paid* for the dog, and it is hers."

Momo forced back her tears and said pleadingly, "Only let me see the Memsahib Lady, and let me see Pempa. Then she will know that he is my dog."

But Gopal looked disdainfully at her.

"You are crazy!" he snorted. "Do you think I could send a little wood rat like you into the presence of the Paton Lady Memsahib? No one can be passed through the doors who does not bring a letter or a card. Go away! It is unseemly for us to allow you to stand here talking to us!"

"If you don't let me go in, I will lie down on the road and scream," said Momo desperately.

"Oh, ho!" replied Gopal fiercely. "Then I will crush you like butter. I will give you to the policeman over there on the corner, and he will carry you off to the jail for disturbing the peace."

Like a deer before its hunter Momo stood, her eyes glancing everywhere, seeking a way of escape. Then, like the sudden flash of lightning from a monsoon sky, she darted between the guards, across the pavement, and was running up the broad steps before they could snatch at her. But the durwans, now really angry, ran after her, leaping up the stairs three at a time. She had her hand on the great door when Gopal caught her, and shook her as a cat shakes a mouse.

"O daughter of a thousand devils! With a peacock's pride and stubborn as an ass! What owl's folly makes you think that you, a wandering wood rat like you—" he shook her angrily again, "could ever, even if granted entrance, pass in at the front, the Sahib's door?"

All his kindness was forgotten now. This hill brat was really a nuisance. Only suppose she had got inside the house, and by the door of ceremony too! and against his clear orders! What then? Gopal had an enemy in the house. The butler looked with envious eyes upon his job. He was constantly scheming to find some excuse to get *him*, Gopal, discharged, in order to find work for his new son-in-law. Just once let this stupid little girl stray into the house—and Gopal might find himself out begging in the street! Gopal shook her again, and dragged her like a sack of rice down the steps, to dump her at the curb.

Momo struggled indeed; like a fish taken out of water, she gasped and struggled; but she was no match for the wiry little fighter. Suddenly she collapsed. Sinking through his grasp and falling to the ground, she lay in a little heap, crying as if her heart would break. Was this the end of her search—to find and reach the very house where Pempa was imprisoned and there to be shut out? Not even to be able to see him! Nor to plead for him to those who had bought him!

"Oh, Pempa, if only you knew that I am here," she thought desperately. "How quickly you would fight and bite your way through armies of servants to find and come to me!"

But the house was huge, the walls were very thick. Even if she called him with all her strength, he might not hear—or if he heard, he might not find a way to escape to her before the durwans would give her up to that tall policeman who stood in the middle of the street, before the palace gates. So Momo lay and wept. Not gently, but in great tearing sobs that shook her whole strong little body, that made her throat and her stomach ache with their violence, she cried.

A big black motor car, shiny and splendid, came purring up to the curb, and stopped before the house. Momo did not see it. The great door of the house opened, and Momo did not know it. From inside the mansion came a murmur of voices, the stir of movement. Momo did not hear it. But the durwans heard and saw. Glancing nervously up the stairs, Gopal saw Abdul, the dignified head bearer, come through the door and bow his mistress out of the house. Already the procession was moving down the steps, first the head bearer, then the Lady Paton, and last her personal attendant, very grand in his red coat, with its brass buttons, and the royal insignia of Government like a huge brass ornament at his belt. Now under their mistress's eye both durwans wanted to be seen zealously carrying out their duties of guarding the doorway of the house. They lifted their sticks and their voices with a great show of fierceness.

"O Tibetan beggar! Go away! *Jao!*" cried Gopal, poking at Momo.

"Away! Go away!" echoed Rama, brandishing his stick and looking ferociously at the little heap at his feet. Still Momo lay like one deaf and blind, and still she sobbed.

Lady Paton stopped and looked down pityingly at Momo.

"What is the matter with her?" she asked the durwans. "Is she lost?"

Her musical voice pierced the child's grief-stopped ears like the silvery chiming of the caravan bells. Momo jumped up, guessed at one glance that this tall English lady was the Burra Memsahib, and prostrated herself at her feet. Then with clasped hands she looked up at her, and still struggling with her sobs, the tears pouring down her cheeks, begged her: "O lady! Shining like the lamps of the sky! Give me back my dog—my Pempa! He is mine, he is mine!"

"What does she say?" asked Lady Paton, touched and wondering. Not a word that Momo spoke was intelligible to her, but she knew children, and understood misery. She did not need words to feel the agony in Momo's heart; and was too kindhearted not to wish to relieve her suffering.

The two durwans looked at each other, and could not quite make up their minds whether or not to tell her the truth. Momo kept on looking pleadingly at Lady Paton, and repeating over and over, "Please give him back to me! Please!'"

"She seems to want something of me," murmured Lady Paton, puzzled. Then to Gopal, and in a tone of firm command, she said, "Tell me what she says—the truth, mind!'"

Now Gopal did not want to tell the truth. It would be much pleasanter for his mistress if he could invent some tale of Momo's grief, and get her sent away with a beggar's dole. But he knew that these English folk worshiped Truth as a god, and preferred always to hear the bitterest truths, no matter how hard for themselves, than the most golden lies. He had learned by experience that they punished more severely for the telling of lies than any other kind of misdeed. Moreover, with Abdul the butler forever watching him like a crow to find a fault and report it, Gopal knew that any lie he might tell would certainly be found out. Besides, in this case the truth could not hurt him. His only connection with the dog had been that matter of the fee he and Rama had taken from Nema Doorg. And he had gone back to the hills. Therefore Gopal told the truth.

"She tells a ridiculous tale," he said, "of having come all the way down from the boundaries of Bhotiyal, over the top of the Jelep La pass, alone, to find her dog, which she says was stolen from her and brought down here and sold to your ladyship."

"*What* did you say?" exclaimed Lady Paton. "This little child came *alone* all that long way, and has found her way here! Is it possible?"

The two durwans tilted their heads to the right, and looked unwinkingly at her out of their slantwise black eyes.

"She says it is so," replied Gopal. "I told her, 'Go home, little girl, for our Memsahib has paid much money for the dog, and it is now hers.' At that the child fell to the ground, and like a cow that has lost its calf, she is wailing."

Lady Paton looked very thoughtful. "Could it be true?" she murmured. "It was only two days ago, surely, that those traders brought me that terrier." She looked intently down at Momo's round brown face, and her pleading black eyes, then came to a sudden decision.

"Let us take her to the top of the stairs, and inside the hall," she commanded. So the little procession climbed the stairs, first the attendant, then the Lady Paton, followed by the two durwans, with Momo in a maze of hope and wonder between them. The attendant threw open the door, and stood aside to let Lady Paton enter. One by one the others filed in after her, and stood in a little group in the great hall.

"Now tell her to call her dog," said Lady Paton. "He is upstairs, not tied, and if indeed he is her dog, he will surely know her call, and come to her." Gopal turned to Momo.

"O favored child! Blessed beyond your merits!" he said. "Call now your dog."

Momo's face brightened like the sun bursting suddenly out from under heavy gray clouds. She threw back her head, opened her mouth round and wide, and her call, free, full-throated, pulsed through the air.

"Pem-pa! Pem-pa-a-a! O Pem-pa-a-a!"

How many times had she stood in her high hills, listening to this cry beat through the clear air like the wings of a bird! And following it in her imagination until it reached Pempa where he wandered. Then how like a flash of sunlight he flew to her side! Here, in this hot and heavy air of Bengal, closed in by the thick walls of this great house, the call seemed to rise and hit the roof, and be thrown back upon them, standing in the hall below. Still "Pempa-a!" went ringing through the house, waking echoes, startling the household. From every direction the household servants came running, their bare feet noiseless on the marble floors. They gathered in a little group at the end of the hall, peeping out at their mistress, whispering to each other, curious.

The first notes of Momo's voice struck upon the sensitive ears of Pempa, where he lay listlessly upon an upper verandah, his head between his paws. His ears pricked up, he lifted his head, and shook the golden mane that fell over his eyes. What dream was this of home and the sweet forests, where above the murmur of the trees and the rush of the rapid streams this adored voice would summon him to his mistress's side? Again that cry—"Pem-pa-a!" This was no dream, the voice was real. *She* was here, and calling him home!

He sprang to his feet, and whining, whimpering, crying in little yelps, and with hope and grief so long endured, he came rushing to the call. The little party waiting in the hall heard his cries, heard too a scampering, a tapping of nails on the marble floor. Then a golden ball shot down the stairs and into Momo's arms. Pempa leaped up at her again and again, and put his forepaws upon her shoulders. He danced and pranced and whirled round and round the hall in circles, in a very frenzy of joy. Then he came up breathless to Momo, throwing back his head, tossing his golden mane so that his black eyes shone out on her, radiant, gleaming with joy. He bared his white teeth in a laugh. He wagged his tail until the long gold hairs of that plume were a tossing, confused tangle.

Momo stood watching his mad antics, laughing and crying together, until suddenly she felt weak from joy and excitement. She sank to the floor and sat there, hugging Pempa to her, her

black head close to his golden one, her arms tight about him, as if never again would she let him go. Pempa, still quivering with his excitement, licked her face and hands with his pink tongue.

All this time Lady Paton had stood staring. The durwans

stared; and from both sides of the hall, the entire staff of a dozen servants, in their white uniforms and red belts and turban bands, stood staring.

"Amazing! Perfectly extraordinary!" Lady Paton murmured to herself. "If I had not seen it with my own eyes I should never have believed it possible." She shook her head, as if to blow away cobwebs, and then remembered the engagement to which she had been going when she met Momo. Hurriedly she turned to leave, but first she spoke to Gopal.

"Keep her here until I get back, Gopal," she said. "I want to hear her story. Take her to your *godown* (room), and let the dog stay with her. Feed her and treat her well, and bring her to see me when the Sahib and I have finished our lunch. I will send for you."

"All right, Memsahib," replied Gopal, saluting smartly. He gave a quick order to the hall boy, standing near, and ran with Rama lightly down the steps ahead of their mistress, to see her safely into her car. They both saluted again as she drove off, then Rama stayed alone to guard the house, while Gopal went after Momo. He found her sitting just as he had left her, still hugging Pempa to her heart.

"Come, child," he said kindly. "The Burra Memsahib says you are to be fed, and to wait in my godown until she comes back to hear the story of your journey to Calcutta."

Momo jumped gladly to her feet, suddenly aware of how hungry she was, and with Pempa still frolicking at her side went out by a servants' circular stairway at the back of the house, and across the garden, to a long line of little houses, where the servants lived. And Gopal, who had himself a little daughter about Momo's age, living with her mother in a village of Nepal, made her tea, and fed her well. Then Momo lay on the ground under a pipul tree, and slept, with her arms about Pempa, who nestled close beside her. She wakened only when Gopal shook her by the shoulder and said, "Come now, Momo, the Burra Memsahib and the Burra Sahib himself will see you." And he led her into the house, and upstairs, and out on to a wide verandah, where the Lady Paton sat beside a tall gentleman on a couch.

Momo bowed and stuck out her tongue, and stood waiting in deep respect. Both Sir Hugh and Lady Paton looked at her in a friendly way and smiled, and Lady Paton spoke eagerly.

"Here she is, Hugh," she said. "See what a little girl! Can you believe that a child the age of our Nancy could make such a journey *alone?* Coming over the mountains, down into a foreign country—and a city the size of Calcutta—without guides or money!"

"Amazing," he replied. "She has courage."

"But," his wife continued, "she not only comes into this confusing foreign country, and a great city, the second largest city in the Empire, where there are people from all over the world. The very first thing she does when she reaches Calcutta—for, remember, she arrived only this morning—the first thing she does is to make her way directly to the people who sold us the dog, and from them to us! Fancy that! It is a miracle!"

"Ah, yes, it is astonishing," her husband replied. "But then you must remember this, my dear: the very fact that there are so many different kinds of people here, and that they all wear their own distinctive dress, makes it easier. Far simpler here than at home in London, for instance. Everyone in Calcutta, looking at this child, would know by her dress and face that she is a Tibetan. There are only a few shops and hostels where the Tibetans who come into the city go to trade and stop. As soon therefore as she ran across someone who could speak her language, she would be directed to these places—and there you are!"

"I still think it miraculous," his wife replied. "What does she say, durwan? Tell us her story, and mind you give it word for word— I want to hear it *all.*"

So Momo told her story, bit by bit, and Gopal repeated it faithfully to the interested couple on the couch. She began, very cunningly, by telling them how she had first got Pempa, and of Dawa the astrologer's prophecy that he would bring them adventures and good fortune; for, she thought, if these English knew that Pempa was hers by the grace of the Blessed One, they would surely give him back to her.

"And therefore," she explained, bowing gravely to Sir Hugh and Lady Paton, "it is by the will of the precious Lord that we meet here today. We have been drawn by the bonds of our former deeds."

Sir Hugh and Lady Paton nodded, and she plunged into the telling of her story. Everyone in the East, from babies to old men and women, loves both to tell and to hear a good story. And Momo talked now as never before, for Pempa was at stake.

She told them of the mists and the night at Gnatong, and how she had been frightened by the yaks and the spirits of the British dead; of the kind women in the tea shops, and the rude one at Lingtam; of the thief at Rongli, and how Little Dorje had saved her; of how she had followed the ten traders to Kalimpong, and the sad story of Tsu Foo, who gave her shelter for the night.

"Oh, poor child!" cried Lady Paton. "What an utterly *beastly* thing to do to a child! We must stop that, Hugh." And her husband nodded.

When they heard of the Lat Sahib's meeting her, and giving her the money for the train fare, Sir Hugh and Lady Paton looked at each other, and Lady Paton exclaimed in surprise.

"Christopher Bates! So it was good old Christopher who gave her the money for the journey! But fancy her meeting *him* —our old friend—just there at the railway station! It's more and more amazing. You must give her a letter, Hugh, to take back to him."

"Rather," her husband replied with a smile. "Carry on, child, I must be off soon."

So Momo, gathering speed, told of the theft of her money, of meeting the young Tibetan priest, of finding the shop of Wing Fong the Chinese, and being helped into his rickshaw by his kind children. Then, having brought herself to the end of her search, she bowed her head, and spoke fervently, with clasped hands.

"She says," repeated Gopal, " 'O Burra Memsahib! Your lovely face shines like the moon on the fifteenth day! I beg you catch me, worthless fish as I am, on your hook of mercy. Give me back my dog—as alms to the poor give him back to me.' "

Before Lady Paton could reply, Momo quoted a Buddhist proverb, imitating the high droning voice of a priest. And then, having as she thought put the greatest possible pressure on these English by reminding them of their religious duty to be generous, she stood still with clasped hands, and looked anxiously at them.

"She says," Gopal translated, " 'The giving of alms to the poor is a most important duty, for wealth collected by avarice, like the honey collected by honey bees, is of no use to one's self.' That is Buddhist talk," he finished. Sir Hugh and Lady Paton smiled at each other and at Momo.

"Yes, yes, of course she shall have her dog," said Lady Paton. "Tell her so at once, Gopal. I can't bear to keep her in suspense."

But Momo guessed her meaning, and without waiting for Gopal's translation, she fell to the floor, prostrating herself before the Lady Paton. Tears of joy rolled silently down her cheeks, and she shook them out of her shining eyes. Then she jumped to her feet, and burst into thanks.

"Victory to thee, O lady! Brilliant above one hundred thousand lights! O diamond comforter of my heart! May your life, body, and power increase like the growing new moon. Great mercy you have shown me. I am thankful. May all good befall you!"

Here Gopal cut her short. "Enough, enough, child!" He shook his head reprovingly at her. "These English have many great affairs and much business to do. They cannot sit all day listening while you endlessly sing the same song, like a cuckoo in spring." Nevertheless, he retold her thanks to his master and mistress, and virtuously added his warning. Sir Hugh rose and smiled down at Momo.

"I'll write a letter now to Christopher," he told his wife, "and send it here. You can deal with the rest, my dear. Good luck, little Momo!" And he was off.

"Tell her, Gopal," Lady Paton said, "that we will give her money for the tickets. She is to stop at Kalimpong to give a letter to the Lat Sahib of Sikkhim. He is our friend." All this Momo heard, and nodded.

"As for Tsu Foo," Lady Paton went on, "she is to go to the home of my friend, Christy Memsahib, on the tea estate near Darjeeling. Christy Memsahib will take good care of her, and train her to do ayah's work. I would have her here with me," she went on, "but Tsu Foo will keep stronger in the hills than here on the hot plains. All this will be in the letter to the Lat Sahib, and his men will arrange everything."

Again Momo nodded, in understanding, but did not look entirely satisfied. And Lady Paton, guessing the reason, went on with a smile, "As for the uncle, Momo, he will be put out of the house, and the Lat Sahib will make Tsu Foo a ward of the state. Her own house will be carefully managed for her until Tsu Foo is old enough to marry and go there to live and run the little tea shop herself." At that good news, Momo's face lighted in a happy smile, and she joined her hands and bowed and bowed in thankfulness.

"O lady! Surpassing the goddesses in beauty!" she cried, in spite of Gopal's gestures, warning her not to waste time by more talk. "As merciful as you are great. Thank you, thank you!"

Lady Paton looked thoughtful, and tapped her fingers on the arm of her couch, then smiled as at some pleasant thought, and said gaily, "And now we must make the second part of the prophecy come true, Momo. You have had your adventures; now we must give you good fortune to carry back to your home." Momo held her breath and looked at her eagerly, quite overwhelmed with blessings.

"Tell your father," said Lady Paton, "that he need no longer risk his life in carrying the mails over the Jelep La pass. The Lat Sahib will see that he is given work either with the wool trade in Rinchengong, or more probably, as caretaker of one of the new dak bungalows the Indian Government is now having built along the line of travel in your country of Tibet."

When Momo heard these words, she prostrated herself again and again on the floor, and murmured her thanks, tears of happiness swimming in her eyes. Lady Paton smiled at her happiness, then frowned, and went on.

"And as for Nema Doorg, the thief," she said, "he **must** learn that no man can prosper by theft. The Lat Sahib will send him an order to find me another Lhasa terrier. He must buy, and not steal it, and bring it here to me when next he comes down to Calcutta."

Gopal repeated this to Momo, who nodded her head at each sentence, vigorously.

"Tell Momo," she continued, knowing how news travels fast as the wind from mouth to mouth, "to send word to Nema Doorg that the Lat Sahib will not forget, and that he will know whether the new dog is got honestly or by theft. And if again Nema Doorg tries to steal, he will be severely punished."

Again Momo nodded, and thanked her. Then Lady Paton gave her money, and this time Momo had learned her lesson; she would be secret and safe in carrying and spending it. Sir Hugh's letter to the Lat Sahib was brought in, and Lady Paton gave that to Momo, with one of her own, that she had hastily written.

"Now, Momo" she said, "you have your dog at your side, and good fortune in those letters in your hand. Take care of them all, and God bless you. Perhaps some day, when I come on a holiday through the hills, we may meet at the bungalow where your father will be caretaker." She stroked Pempa's head. "Good-by, Pempa," she said. "Now I know why you were so unhappy here with me."

Momo prostrated herself again, stuck out her tongue, and bowed herself out of the room.

"Oh, Gopal," Lady Paton called, as he followed Momo out, "be sure to see that Momo has food, and take her to the train tonight, and put her safely on it."

So that evening, when the sun had sunk, a great red ball, into the west, and the quick twilight came, Gopal took Momo to the station. Again she rode in a rickshaw, but this time she had Pempa on her lap, and Gopal sat at her side. And in the blue light of the evening she looked again at the city. Gopal spoke to the rickshaw coolie as they started, and he carried them round the corner past the Government House, skirted another large park, and came out upon a broad road running beside the river. Before them was a *ghat* (water stairs) for bathing. The mighty river flowed dark and quick, and there were many yellow lights on the water from the boats anchored or moving there. The rickshaw coolie stopped, resting his arms, and Gopal turned to Momo.

"O daughter of the hills!" he said. "Look now, and it may be for the last time in your life, upon our Mother Ganges. Whoever bathes in her holy waters washes away all sin; but even those who look will gain merit. See! Is there anything, even in the land of the high hills and the snow peaks, so marvelous?"

"Lah-se!" Momo breathed, for in this half darkness the lustrous dark river with its twinkling lights was even more majestic than by sunlight. "It is truly a marvel!"

"Indeed, yes," replied Gopal, gratified to see her wonder. And in the tone of one who confers a great favor he added, "Out of the straight path to the Sealdah Station have we come here, child, for I thought it not good to let you depart from the plains without even a glance at our Mother Ganges. We go now to the train."

The coolie trotted off again, taking them first through wide and handsome streets lined by great houses, big as palaces, and large shops, whose fronts were all of glass. Then they came into narrower, crowded streets such as she had passed through that morning, and finally to the bazaars, still open and lighted by yellow flares, or sometimes electric lights. And following a street which took a curving way through the city they came at last to the station. Here they left the rickshaw, and Gopal led Momo through the confusion of traffic, into the great station, and up to the ticket booth. Momo handed him the money she had taken out of her pouch while still in the rickshaw, and he got her a ticket.

"Hold it carefully!" he warned, and led the way out along the tracks to where the Up Darjeeling Mail lay, taking on its passengers. Stopping before one third-class carriage which was not yet overcrowded, Gopal spoke in a lordly way to the people sitting there.

"O travelers! This child of the hills goes to Siliguri under the protection of the Burra Lat Sahib. Let no one touch nor harm her or her dog, but show her at Siliguri how she should get a ticket for Giellekhola."

And all the people looked at the red bands on his turban and his belt, and the brass buttons on his coat, and nodded their heads respectfully, and said, "*Accha* (All right). It shall be so." So they made room for Momo and Pempa to sit among them. She thanked Gopal, and he went off. Soon the warning bell rang for the train, and it began to glide quietly ("like a snake," Momo told herself in surprise) out of the station.

She sat with her arms tight around Pempa, who every now and then raised his face to look at her, and licked her hands with his pink tongue. For a time she looked out of the window, at these vast flat plains, where the palm trees rustled against a dark blue sky, and the stars shone in the waters of the square pools, and the little villages were dark and silent. The train wheels sang their continuous refrain: "*Click,* click, click, click! *Click,* click, click, click!"

To this song Momo fell asleep, while the train carried her and Pempa farther and farther north, away from the flat plains of Bengal, and nearer and nearer to their cool hills. And whenever they stopped at the up-country stations, she wakened to the joy of feeling her own treasure Pempa safe in her arms, and tucked securely into her bloused robe the letters which were to bring good fortune to her family and to Tsu Foo.

Mangalam! All happiness!

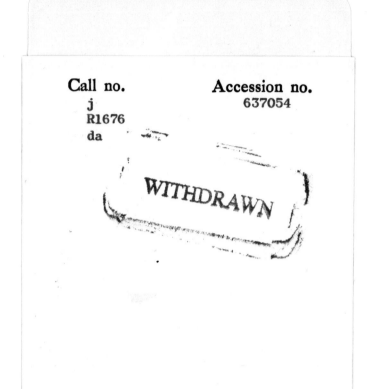